POWER

★REAL ESTATE★

LISTING

WILLIAM H. PIVAR

with photographs by Corinne E. Pivar, API

While a great deal of care has been taken to provide accurate and current information, the ideas, suggestions, general principles, and conclusions presented in this book are subject to local, state, and federal laws and regulations, court cases, and any revisions of same. The reader is thus urged to consult legal counsel regarding any points of law—this publication should not be used as a substitute for competent legal advice.

© 1983 by Development Systems Corporation

Published by Real Estate Education Company/Chicago,
a subsidiary company of Longman Group Limited

Printed in the United States of America

83   84   85   10   9   8   7   6   5   4   3   2   1

Library of Congress Cataloging in Publication Data

Pivar, William H.
    Power real estate listing.

    1. Real estate listings.   2. Real estate business.
3. Real estate agents.   I. Title.
HD1382.6.P58   1983   333.33'068'8   82-24108
ISBN 0-88462-480-3

Contents

To my partner, my pal, my wife

Special thanks to the following people, whose constructive
manuscript reviews contributed so much to this book:
Roger Reitzel, Director of Training, Quinlan and Tyson,
Schaumburg, Illinois.
Ruth Williams, Director of Training, Byrnes, Barroll & Gaines
Realtors, Inc., Towson, Maryland.
David R. Stipp, Tustin, California

Introduction

A few real estate licensees achieve phenomenal success in getting listings. This elite group does not really compete with the herd of salespeople who badger owners of advertised For Sale By Owner property. The truly successful few obtain many of their listings long before they see a For Sale sign on the property or a By Owner ad in the newspaper. They have found a better way to go.

This book reveals the successful salesperson's secrets of finding listings, traditional and nontraditional. It opens up dozens of unworked listing sources as well as techniques for recognizing additional listing opportunities in unexpected places.

With the Power Listing approach, locating property is only the first step. Power Listing uses a group of highly structured techniques—direct-planned presentations designed to turn listing possibilities into probabilities. The direct, rational Power approaches make it difficult for an owner to say "no," but easy to say "yes."

This book spells out ways to improve applications of conventional listing techniques as well as to use highly effective innovative approaches. It shows how understanding the owner's needs and wants prepares the licensee to sell him- or herself to the owner. By teaching the salesperson to uncover the "Why?" of owner objections, *Power Real Estate Listing* prepares the licensee to overcome objections, turning negative beginnings into positive conclusions.

Despite all the courses and training sessions salespeople undertake in hopes of learning to obtain listings, very few see the importance of going for quality. A poor-quality listing cannot compete on price and terms with available alternative properties. The poor-quality listing is worse than worthless. It demands time and money and offers little promise of a successful sale. This book explains in detail how to convert what would ordinarily be a below-average or average listing into a generator of buyer excitement.

A good inventory is the first requirement for any merchant's survival. The real estate brokerage operates under the same law: having a good stock-in-trade of quality listings is essential for success.

A real estate salesperson who can list well will build a successful career, since listing requires greater sales skills than selling property. Property selling has the advantage of a tangible that can be seen, felt and walked through. Getting a listing means selling an intangible: your own ability. The first sale in any real estate transaction consists of selling an owner on your representation. This book will prepare you to master that difficult but essential skill.

1

Getting Organized

For many of us, a cartoon sums up our approach to life: "Next week we've got to get organized." For the person in real estate, next week is right now. Nothing gets done without planning and organization. Organizing for real estate success demands both physical and mental preparation. This chapter describes the details and techniques of each.

THE RIGHT TOOLS

Physical preparation means, among other things, having the right tools. Here are some of the essentials.

Calling Cards. Your card must compete with many others. Ten salespeople might have contacted a For Sale By Owner property seller, each leaving a card. When the owner decides he or she wants professional assistance, which of these salespeople will be chosen? The winning candidate will be the one who has found a way to direct attention to that card, and to ensure that the card and the agent's face are correctly associated in the owner's mind.

Many people try to make their cards memorable by using odd sizes, different colors, fold-out designs or peculiar materials. One aluminum products salesman has cards of sheet aluminum. People remember him.

Other salespeople try to give their cards memorable messages:

MEET TOM HICKS

HE IS GOING TO SELL YOUR HOUSE

Sunshine Realty   *928-1000*
West Hwy 87, Sunshine, Ill.

Some salespeople put a joke, a calendar or an astrological prediction on the backs of their cards, hoping this will persuade people to keep them. Here is a simple, but far more effective, approach: put your photograph on your card. This is the easiest and best way to help people associate your face with your name.

Get in the habit of always carrying plenty of cards in your pocket and in your car. Make sure your friends and relatives all have a generous supply. Here are some ways to use them to put your name before the people who already know you by face, or who have ties to your area:

• When you eat in a restaurant, leave a card with your tip. A note on the card such as: "Thanks for the great service," will add to its effectiveness.

• Leave cards with neighbors, bartenders, service station attendants, repair people, and service personnel you meet.

• When you use a public phone, leave your card in the Yellow Pages under Real Estate.

• When you pass a community bulletin board, put up your card.

• When you mail a check, enclose your card. People who receive money from you are interested in your continued prosperity.

Cards are an effective low-cost way to let others know that you can help them with their real estate needs.

Directories. Along with telephone directories, street directories provide an excellent tool for canvassing, since they give you the name of each home occupant. Reverse directories cover many areas, and computers should soon make them available just about everywhere. With these, you can find out the name and address of a person whose phone number you know. Instead of calling a number from a For Sale By Owner ad like all the other salespeople, you can knock on the door in person, and greet the owner by name.

Amortization Tables. A number of title insurance firms offer free amortization books, essential for determining loan payments. With these books you can quickly tell owners what size payments they will receive if they help finance a buyer. Carry one with you and an extra in your car.

Even better than these free amortization books is the *Realty Bluebook*, which provides quarterly, semiannual and annual payments in addition to monthly schedules. From the tables you can compute the years remaining on a loan if you know the balance, interest rate and monthly payment. You can also compute the amount of a future balloon payment or the present value of future money, based upon different rates of return.

The Bluebook is updated annually to include the latest tax law information. It is available as a pocket-size book or as a full-size copy with much larger print. The *Realty Bluebook* is available from Professional Publishing Corporation, 122 Paul Drive, San Rafael, CA 94903.

Calculator. An inexpensive pocket calculator is something every real estate salesperson should carry at all times. It aids in a

wide variety of calculations—computing an owner's net from
a sale, figuring square footage and acreage, figuring your own
commissions.   Make sure the batteries are changed regularly
or you may get incorrect totals.

Mastering a more sophisticated hand calculator such as
the Texas Instruments Business Analyst II will enable you to
dispense with the amortization tables and the Realty Bluebook described above.   Your use of these advanced devices
to provide financial answers will also impress clients with
your professional expertise.

Files. You should keep a file on each of your own listings, with up-
to-date records of all owner contacts and showings, plus multiple listing sheets and copies of all ads for each property.

Sold and expired listings.   A master file on sold and
expired listings from your office and your multiple listing
service can be invaluable in locating comparables for listing
appraisals. If you have an office computer, this data can be
entered for quick retrieval.

Prospects.   You should have a file on every prospective
seller, with cards showing each contact made, your comments, and information on seller motivation.

Listing clauses.   A file of listing clauses for special purposes should be kept with your listing presentation material,
allowing you to quickly handle unusual situations.   As an
aid to preparing these special clauses, go through your old
office listings.   Many offices have created their own "Book
of Clauses" as a permanent reference tool.

Tickler.   A daily tickler file will indicate calls to be made
or information to be checked.   Some salespeople like a huge
calendar with large daily blocks for such information. Use
one of these systems to note listing expirations about 20
days before the end date. If you trust to memory, chances
are your trust will be misplaced.

Phone Aids. Have a printed telephone solicitation presentation on
your desk under plastic or glass. Get in the habit of following your phone solicitation verbatim.

It is a good idea to put one of those little smiling happy face stickers on your phone to remind you to smile as you talk. Some firms specializing in telephone sales place mirrors on each desk so salespeople can see themselves as they make their presentations. Mirrors serve as a reminder to convey a pleasant image.

Your Car. You need wheels if you are going to list real estate. This doesn't mean you must have a luxury car, although many real estate people do.

Some people need a luxury car to prove their importance to themselves and others. Generally, luxury cars will not help you unless you list very expensive property and/or deal with people who are very successful. Successful people do like to deal with other successful people, although a top line Buick or Oldsmobile would probably serve you in this regard as well as would a Mercedes.

One benefit a luxury car does offer is extremely high payments, which serve as excellent motivators for many salespeople. One land sales firm pays for the rental of new Cadillacs for salespeople who reach a particular sales volume. A salesperson who falls below that figure in any month becomes liable for the rental payment. The company says this motivator works, though I hope you can find a better motivator than excessive debt.

A four-door automobile is best for real estate work, as you will frequently have several passengers. Older people often have a hard time getting in and out of the back seat of sporty-looking two-door models.

Whatever kind of car you have, keep it clean. We seldom see our own cars as others do, from the back seat. By sitting in the back seat you may become aware of cleaning deficiencies. Use air fresheners to mask the odors of old tobacco smoke.

A car isn't as important for listings as it is for sales. One California broker uses his motorcycle for listing calls. His ads, signs and cards show a caricature of him driving a motorcycle with a scarf flying behind.

In Your Car. When you get a listing you must be ready to seal the deal. Your car can be a mobile office that keeps you ready for any possibility. Here is a checklist of items to keep permanently in your car.

Extra Telephone Book. An extra telephone book in your car is essential for checking addresses. Public phone booths are often without a book, so having your own can save a great deal of time.

Instant Camera. A Polaroid-type instant camera should be kept in your car along with extra film. This camera can be a valuable tool in obtaining listings, in preparing sample listings for an owner, and in showing comparables. In hot weather carry your camera and film with you, as the heat in your car can damage the film.

Cassette Recorder. A small cassette recorder can be used effectively to take notes of ideas as you drive, to record addresses of For Sale By Owner property, vacant property, rental signs, etc. You can also use it to obtain data for a competitive market analysis.

I recommend that the recorder be used while driving by yourself to record listing presentations. You can then listen to your presentations and critique yourself. Rather than listening to music, you can play tapes that help you develop skills and improve your motivation.

Flashlight. A powerful flashlight with fresh batteries enables you to read addresses and street signs and to show property after dark. Even when the electricity is on, a vacant house may not have ceiling fixtures in every room, or bulbs in what fixtures remain. A fluorescent tube light, the kind used for camping, works quite well for showing or checking on real estate.

Presentation Materials. You should have a listing presentation book (Chapter 4) in your car. Keep another written presentation for canvassing inside your car in a plastic protector. It should be reviewed prior to house-to-house canvassing.

Extra Forms. Keep a heavy plastic envelope under the car seat with extra listing and sales forms and several pencils. Some excellent car files are available at office supply stores.

Rainwear. An umbrella or raincoat and boots should be in your car. The boots are useful for checking raw land as well as putting up signs.

Tape Measure. A 50- to 100-foot tape measure as well as a smaller metal tape measure will allow you to compute square footage accurately and to obtain interior measurements.

Signs. If possible you should carry several For Sale signs and stakes in your car, along with a hammer and nails.

Lock Boxes. Carrying several spare lock boxes in your car will prepare you to begin showing a property as soon as you have a listing agreement. Your preparation will show owners your professionalism.

YOUR APPEARANCE

Just as you want a house to be "standing tall" and looking sharp for a prospective buyer, you should be concerned about your own personal appearance. Your mode of dress should be based upon the area and your clientele. While a three-piece suit would be appropriate in many metropolitan areas, it would make you seem overdressed in many Southwestern towns. You want to look successful, but not to intimidate owners.

On the other hand, casualness can go too far. I met a real estate salesman who drove a pink Cadillac convertible, dressed like a teenage rock star, and had at least a half dozen gold chains around his neck and several rings on both hands, including a large pinky diamond. He looked more like he was selling flesh than real estate. This kind of appearance will not inspire confidence and can lose business for you.

Some real estate saleswomen dress as if they were going to a party at night rather than to work during the day. Overdressing invites negative reactions from other women.

One of my professors at college cautioned us against wearing bow ties. "How can you have any trust in anyone who would wear one of those ridiculous looking things," he asked. We don't see many bow ties around today, but the professor's basic advice was sound. Your dress as well as your manner should be designed to convey your image as a competent professional.

MENTAL PREPARATION

One of the most knowledgeable people I know in real estate was a miserable failure when it came to actually obtaining listings and sales. He now teaches others what he couldn't do himself. He had the knowledge but lacked the drive, the positive motivation, necessary for success.

Positive Motivation. To be successful you must be positively motivated. Most people are affected more by their failures than their successes. They are negatively motivated, believing that since they failed before in similar circumstances, they will fail again. With this attitude, they expend the effort necessary to guarantee failure. Continued failure reinforces their certain knowledge that nothing they do will succeed. Their prophecy of failure becomes self-fulfilling. You may hear people in your office say that "Owners are not interested in selling before Christmas." One saleswoman told me, "In twenty-seven years in real estate, I never took a listing in the two-week period before Christmas." Property is listed in those weeks, but she makes sure they aren't her listings.

Some salespeople start out with a bang, then seem to fade away. Other salespeople say, "He burned himself out." Nobody physically burns out. What happens is that attitudes change as the influence of failures begins to overbalance the encouragement of success. People learn that they cannot succeed in certain situations and act accordingly.

The "dumb" salesperson doesn't learn from his or her failures that success is not possible. The dumb salesperson keeps trying, expecting to succeed, and does succeed. We have all given up on prospects only to find out they bought from someone else who was too dumb to know they wouldn't.

You Are Important. Some salespeople take a "Pardon me" approach. They are apologetic about bothering an owner, failing to realize that they are doing a service by meeting owners' needs. If anyone should jump through hoops on command, it is the owner, not the salesperson. Whether you are knocking on doors or using the phone, you are there for a very important purpose. If you don't regard yourself as a worthwhile person doing important work, no one will.

Some salespeople consistently get the really big sales while others in the same office have to settle for the left-overs. The problem is often one of self-image. A salesperson without high regard for himself or herself does not feel able to deal effectively with important people, and proves the truth of that belief every day. You must fully convince yourself of your value and importance before you can convince others.

Their Best Interest. In dealing with people, keep their best interest uppermost in your mind. Before you can help them you have to convince them. Take the attitude that *no* means *maybe* and *maybe* means *yes.* With this in mind, you can be tenacious in your efforts to serve peoples' needs.

"Luck." Worrying about what others do only depresses you if they outdo you, or makes you complacent if they don't. Strive to improve yourself without regard to either the successes or failures of others.

Some real estate salespeople excuse their own poor performance by crediting others with "luck." It is a strange fact in real estate that the harder a salesperson works and the more knowledge that salesperson obtains, the luckier that person becomes. A great fisherman once told me, "Luck is simply knowledge and opportunity coming together at the same time, usually as the direct result of a lot of hard work."

Role-playing. Failures are failures if you fail to learn from them, but failures can become successes. We have all relived incidents in our lives and considered what we should have said or done. This natural reaction can be controlled to become an excellent learning tool for the salesperson.

Get in the habit of performing a postmortem on your successes as well as your failures. Ask yourself what you did right and what you could have said better. Mentally go through the entire presentation.

Consider what an ideal "supersalesperson" would have said. Imagine owners throwing the worst possible curves at you. How would the supersalesperson answer the owners' questions or objections? This exercise prepares you for actual situations. When you meet a question or objection you have previously considered, you will be prepared to answer in a positive manner. You will have learned to think like this supersalesperson who, in reality, will have become you.

Verbal role-playing between salespeople can be extremely valuable as it trains you to quickly organize your thoughts and express yourself when confronted with the unexpected. Some offices include role-playing situations as part of each regular sales meeting.

By recording your listing presentations and playing them back, you will develop a smooth presentation with effective timing. A saleswoman I know carries a small recorder in her purse. She turns it on whenever she is making a presentation. Then she critiques herself. Before you tape other people, be sure to obtain their permission.

Sales firms know that actors make excellent salespeople. They are accustomed to rehearsing their lines and can accept a script. The salesperson who knows it all but doesn't follow a script fails when he or she gets on center stage. A sales presentation is too important to be ad-libbed without adequate rehearsal.

Goal Setting. Many people who are attracted to real estate seek independence. These people do not want to work under the control of others. What they often fail to realize is that real estate success requires the harshest kind of discipline, self-discipline.

People who are in the habit of taking orders often have great difficulty in setting their own schedules. Their problem is that they have not learned to set goals or to direct their time toward meeting those goals.

Goals are simply road maps to show you where you are now, where you want to be, and what you have to do to arrive at that destination. Without goals you leave to chance what could be achieved by design. It's possible to have many small successes but no overall change. Imagine yourself at the starting line in a race without knowing which way or how far it is to the finish line. Many people spend their entire lives in such races, rushing around and getting nowhere.

Long-term Goals. Long-term goals tell you where the finish line is. To set long-term goals, ask yourself what you hope to be doing in five years, ten years, fifteen years or even twenty years.

Say your ten-year goal is to have multiple real estate offices with a minimum of 100 salespeople working for you. Now this long-term goal will never amount to more than a wish unless you have a map to guide you to it.

Interim Goals. Interim goals are natural steps to a long-term goal. Just as there are different routes on a map that lead to the same destination, career goals are approachable in many ways. Here are two routes, for example, to the multiple offices with 100 salespeople:

ROUTE 1		**ROUTE 2**	
1st year:	I will take and pass the real estate broker's examination.	1st year:	I will take and pass the real estate broker's examination.
2nd year:	I will obtain a position as sales manager for a general real estate brokerage firm.	2nd year:	I will have opened my own general real estate office.
3rd year:	I will have completed an MBA in marketing.	3rd year:	I will have developed a comprehensive training program.

4th year:	I will have completed the requirements for the certified real estate brokerage manager (CRB), designation.	4th year:	I will have established a separate property management department.
5th year:	I will have opened my own office.	5th year:	I will open my first branch office.
6th year:	I will have opened my first branch office.	6th year:	I will establish my own license training program.
7th year:	I will have opened my second branch office.	7th year:	I will open a branch office for investment property and land sales.
8th year:	I will have opened my third branch office.	8th year:	I will have set up a department for business opportunity sales.
9th year:	I will have opened my fourth branch office.	9th year:	I will have developed a division to handle builder tract sales.
10th year:	I will now have a minimum of 100 salespeople working for me at my various offices	10th year:	I will now have a minimum of 100 salespeople working for me at my various offices.

Each of the steps shown is really an interim goal. To be successful, your interim goals should logically lead to your long-term goals. Unrelated accomplishments lead you nowhere.

Definite goals will keep you from becoming sidetracked into temporary situations. It is very easy to remain in the status quo; most people do. Goals force you to look ahead and evaluate your life. Meeting goals will give you satisfaction and positive motivation for further achievements. Goals force changes upon you. While you might set goals and fail to meet them, a plan maximizes your chances for success.

Write down your career goals and interim goals, and show them to people around you. A spouse can be very supportive, and once you have told another person, you will feel obligated to strive for the interim goals. This can be an excellent motivator.

Don't, however, discuss career goals with co-workers. They will tend to laugh or tell you why you are being unrealistic. They are likely drifting career-wise and really don't want you to be successful: that would only make them seem like failures in their own eyes.

Measurable Goals. Your goals should all be measurable so that you cannot delude yourself about whether you've met them. Goals to "improve" or to be "more effective" can't really be measured. Your goals should be objective so you can say, "Yes, they have been met" or "No, they have not been met." Specify a particular number of listings, contacts or success rate so you can definitely evaluate your progress.

Goal Change. Career goals and interim goals should not be cast in concrete. Interests and values change. When you change career goals, you are likely to find that most of your preparation is still valuable. Interim goals are flexible enough to apply to many different career goals.

When you reach your career goal, you will find that you have still further goals. Goal setting is a lifelong effort to strive for something better.

Daily Goals. Daily goals are the rungs upon which you climb to reach your interim and career goals. Each night you should set forth your goals for the following day and evaluate your accomplishments. If any goals were not met, you should find out why. If an unmet goal is still meaningful, include it in the next day's goals.

Some people write very complete plans which are tied to a clock, like the following:

Morning

8:30— 9:00   Check daily papers for listing prospects.

9:00— 9:30   Telephone prospecting from the newspaper.

9:30—10:00   Contact a minimum of five personnel offices for upcoming retirements, transfers, promotions, etc.

10:30—11:30   Listing presentation — J. Dooley

Afternoon

12:00— 1:00   Lunch with Kermit Nelson, Personnel Director, K-Wave Electronics.

1:00— 2:00   Prepare competitive market analysis for Mr. and Mrs. Schmidt.

2:00— 3:00   Check courthouse for divorces, foreclosure actions and bankruptcies.

3:00— 4:00   Initial listing calls based on morning phone calls. If no appointments, canvass the neighborhood of the Newton Street sale for listings.

4:00— 5:00   Return all daily calls. Call at least six previous buyers as to their needs as well as the needs of their friends.

5:00— 6:00   Make calls from prospective buyer file on new listings.

7:00   Show Mr. and Mrs. Taylor the Skylark home.

You will notice that some of these daily goals are merely to spend a period of time at an activity. These are measurable goals. At the end of each day you will easily be able to evaluate your accomplishments.

Realistically, we know that calls and unexpected opportunities can upset plans. Nevertheless, by writing down a daily plan you will get a great deal more productive work done than if you had no goals at all.

Think about the salespeople in your office. How much of their time is spent really productively? An analysis will probably show that they spend one or two hours a day in office bull sessions or on the phone. They probably have long lunches and coffee breaks with other salespeople. They go to see listings they have little chance of selling. In the evening, they probably socialize with other salespeople.

In my experience, a full-time salesperson who spends four hours a day in productive work is above-average.

• The average real estate salesperson does not set daily goals and evaluate their completion, preferring to be loose to take advantage of situations as they develop.

• The average real estate salesperson does not feel a need for additional professional education, but believes that what is needed is a better market.

• The average real estate salesperson complains about bad business, bad owners and bad buyers.

• The average real estate salesperson is not a successful real estate salesperson.

You are in a business with more unsuccessful people than successful ones—don't join the majority. From your daily goals you will see that there are more productive things to do than there is time to accomplish them. You will find ways to utilize small blocks of time, making each minute an asset instead of an empty period to fill.

If your daily goals lead you to your interim goals and the interim goals lead you to your career goals, then success doesn't have to be just a daydream.

2
Where to Find Listing Prospects

A few listings do walk in the front door, but don't count on them. Generally you will have to beat the bushes, and you will find that there are a great many bushes to beat. There are two ways to be successful at real estate: one is to do what others are doing, only better; the other is to follow your own path and do what others fail to do. Both of these approaches can work if they are done right. This chapter will discuss listing sources, some familiar and some you've never considered, and how to approach them for best results.

LOOK FOR MOTIVATION

It has been said that everything has its price. Property is no exception. Owners can be persuaded to put property on the market when they really don't want or need to dispose of it: if they are promised enough, they will agree to sell. Such owners will never become motivated sellers. They will reject reasonable offers that motivated sellers would have jumped at.

The more motivated the seller, the greater the likelihood that the property can be competitively listed and that a reasonable offer will be accepted. You can logically expect the greatest success if you concentrate your efforts on listings from highly motivated sellers. There are enough people who really need your help to keep you from trying to convince unmotivated owners to sell.

How do you identify the motivated seller? Here is a short field guide to the varieties of prospects, and the characteristics to look for.

STRONG MOTIVATION

1. Purchased another home and having difficulty making two payments.

2. Job transfer and forced to leave area.

3. Personal problems requiring cash.

4. Imminent foreclosure.

5. Emotional or health reasons to leave the area.

MEDIUM MOTIVATION

1. Desire for a nicer, larger or smaller home.

2. Desire to live in a better or more convenient location. (If there are serious problems in the present area this may be a strong motivation.)

3. Desire for housing with less maintenance.

LOW MOTIVATION

1. Willingness to sell for a specific profit.

2. Lack of need or specific desire to change locations.

PROSPECTING IN THE NEWSPAPERS

Soon after the morning papers were delivered, real estate

offices where I worked looked like school libraries before final exams. Every desk would be covered with printed pages that serious-faced salespeople studied with scholarly zeal. A quick survey, however, shattered any illusions about a dedicated sales force mapping out its strategy. The vast majority of the papers were opened to the sports section or the crossword puzzle, followed naturally by the Help Wanted ads.

A few salespeople did work the For Sale By Owner ads before settling down to a morning with the sports pages. As far as I know, no one ever did sell a condo to a quarterback or list a shortstop's house.

Not that the ambitious salesperson should stick with the Classifieds: far from it. The news pages of the paper offer a potential treasure trove of listing clues to those who know what to look for and how to make use of what they find. Phone calls based on detective work in the newspaper have thousands of times greater chances for success than do cold phone canvasses. This section gives details on what to look for in your daily paper, and proven ways to follow up on the leads you uncover.

Marriages and Engagements. These announcements are an excellent source for both listings and sales. Note especially the ages of the bride and groom. If this is a second marriage, one or both parties may have a surplus home or one that does not meet family needs. Many single people also own houses and condos.

Checking the address in the phone book and city directory will determine whether the bride and groom live with parents. If not, do they live in areas of single-family homes, condominium projects or mobile home parks? If so, they are likely to be owners.

Because of the economics of two incomes, marriage can mean two dwellings being sold and a larger or more luxurious home being purchased. In other cases homes will be sold because one or both spouses might feel uncomfortable living in a unit formerly occupied by a divorced or deceased spouse.

    Parents. Besides the married couple providing listings, the parents of the bride and groom are likely prospects to sell. Empty nesters often decide on a smaller home, an apartment, or even to retire to another area. An especially good listing source is single parents. When their last child has left, they often feel lost in a home by themselves. Upkeep becomes a problem without anyone to share it with.

    Some churches post the banns. This is the formal announcement of the upcoming wedding, usually found in the church's newsletter.

Births. Births are a joyous reason to sell. Check the addresses of the parents. For parents living in condominiums or mobile home parks, a birth will often result in a sale in order to purchase family-type housing. Births can also mean the need for larger housing units.

Deaths. Most real estate salespeople avoid following up on death notices, bypassing a good source of listings and a chance to perform a real and needed service for people in difficult times. Worse yet, they leave the field to salespeople who may utilize this source in a callous manner without consideration or understanding of the owners' feelings.

    Some real estate agents send out sympathy cards to people they never met and with whom they have nothing in common. They include their business card, or even a personal note to make it appear that they were friends of the deceased. In England, the National Association of Estate Agents considers this ghoulish approach to be unethical, and I fully agree with them. Another sorry evidence of insensitivity is the practice of knocking on doors almost before the deceased is in the grave. Contacting a surviving spouse or heir while he or she is in an emotional state of shock cannot be condoned.

    Nevertheless, there are many reasons an heir or surviving spouse may find it best to sell property. The financial burden may be too much to bear alone, or the physical problems of maintaining the property may be too great. How, then, can you offer your advice and service to the survivors in a humane and ethical manner?

If you had a relationship with the deceased—a business relationship or membership in the same lodge—a note expressing sympathy and offering help and advice is appropriate. *Do not* include a business card.

I talked to a saleswoman who works only death notices. Her approach is to canvass in the area where the deceased lived about two weeks after the death. She asks neighbors who might be interested in selling or who had a change in family size. When she hears of a death, she asks, "Do you think Mrs. Weiss might be interested in knowing the current value of her property? It could help her in making any decisions." The answer to a question worded in this manner is likely to be positive, since she is offering help.

Her approach to the surviving spouse is:

"Mrs. Weiss, your neighbor Sylvia Wright suggested that I contact you. I am Phyllis King with Continent Realty. Mrs. Wright thought that you would be interested in knowing the current market value of your home in order to help you make any decisions you might be considering. I would be glad to prepare a competitive market analysis for you without cost or obligation. This will provide you with an up-to-date analysis of what your home would bring at a sale should you decide to sell it. In times of great stress I don't recommend any hasty decisions, but knowing the market value can help you to make a decision."

When she gets a positive response or a "Well, I don't know," she continues:

"Would it be all right if I looked through your home and asked you several questions?"

When she presents the competitive market analysis, she doesn't press for the listing. She does not want to press the owner into a decision not in the owner's best interests. She told me that by the time she presents her competitive market analysis the owner will usually have made up his or her own mind.

Normally in real estate transactions, the involvement of relatives means disaster. This is usually not the case if there has been a death. Children will often recommend that the parent sell and either move in with them or move to an apartment or to a retirement community.

In handling listings from death notices, convey that you are there to help in any way you can, and if the owner decides that a sale is in his or her best interest, then you will help. View your role as educational, explaining market value, owner financing, and other necessary information.

Graduations. Graduation often means children leaving home, changing a family's housing requirements. Parents no longer need as much space, or the high utility costs that go with it. This is especially true in the case of single parents.

Graduation also affects families economically. Parents are relieved of a tremendous financial burden when a child graduates from college. A son or daughter in a private college or professional school can cost over $10,000 per year, with no tax benefits. Parents often consider moving up in housing or a change in lifestyle once the obligation of a child's education has been fulfilled.

Divorces. Divorce cuts the number of people occupying a household and often has adverse financial repercussions on the parties. Homes must often be sold for divorce settlements. When one spouse gets the home, income and support and/or alimony may not suffice to maintain that lifestyle. Homes are frequently sold in favor of more modest housing.

After a divorce many people look to other areas for a fresh start. They may desire to return to an area where they once lived, to return to their parents' hometown, or to go someplace where they have always wanted to live.

Besides notices of divorce, check the personal columns in the newspaper with its "Not responsible for . . ." ads which indicate separations. Divorce information is also available as a matter of public record at your county courthouse. I recommend that contacts in cases of divorce be handled as discussed under Deaths.

Promotions. Promotions mean greater income. People's homes today reflect their economic standing much more than in past years. Improved income means a desire for status housing, as well as the better lifestyle that goes with stepping up in housing.

Transfers. People receiving job transfers to other areas usually must sell their homes. Since they need housing where they are going, they make good candidates for relocation referrals to other brokers.

Firms Closing. When a firm goes out of business for any reason, it affects the lives of its employees at every level. While some find positions in the area, others leave.

Highly paid and specialized personnel are the most likely to relocate. Besides housing sales, a firm's closing could mean listings of the firm's real estate. While the financial pages will provide information on larger firms closing their doors, Going Out of Business sales are often found in retail advertisements.

Takeovers. When one firm acquires another, the firm taken over usually undergoes many personnel changes. Often a firm's functions are transferred to a corporate headquarters, which means the termination or transfer of personnel. Besides selling homes for people transferred or otherwise displaced, the corporate real estate officer should be contacted. There is a good chance that he or she will have surplus property to dispose of. Your stockbroker will likely have corporate addresses and even phone numbers of the acquiring business.

Construction Notices. Newspapers often list building permits taken out for new commercial or industrial facilities. This can mean there will be surplus facilities when the construction is completed.

Rental Ads. When a single-family home is offered for rent, you can assume that the owners cannot, or fear they cannot, sell it. People trying to rent their houses should be contacted and informed of the dangers and difficulties involved, and the ways you may be able to help with a sale.

A home rental ad that indicates the owner will give a lease option should be regarded as a cry for help. The owner wants to sell. It is far superior to a For Sale By Owner ad because you know the owner is really motivated. Few real estate salespeople follow up on these ads, while dozens call on the For Sale By Owner ads.

Any time a rental ad sounds desperate it should be followed up. This is the case in many vacant commercial buildings where freebies such as several months' rent and/or moving expenses are offered. The more desperate an owner is to rent, the more likely he or she will be willing to sell.

Personal Property Sales. Advertisements for distress sales of personal property such as stereos, sporting equipment, etc. often mean a person has financial problems. A telephone solicitation call could well result in a listing.

Trades. People advertising that they will trade often want to sell but may have been unable to do so. With maximum capital gains now only 20 percent and the new rapid depreciation laws, trades no longer provide the benefits they once did. In most cases owners come out ahead by selling the property and then buying investment property which they can depreciate. By educating them to this fact, you might obtain a listing.

Some owners advertising trades are really out to steal. They have inflated the value of their property in the hope of finding an unsophisticated trading partner. These owners are not highly motivated, and will seldom list at a competitive price.

For Sale By Owner. You should regard a For Sale By Owner sign, ad or notice on a bulletin board as a cry for help. Usually the owner is motivated to sell but has no idea what selling involves, which explains why so few owners are able to sell their homes at a fair price and terms.

Owners often try to sell their real estate by putting up a 3″ by 5″ card describing their property on a bulletin board at the local market, laundromat or community center. Some even include a photograph. Many of these notices are for property not advertised in the newspapers, or even with a For Sale sign.

As a professional, you are a problem solver. A sale is a solution to a problem. The next chapter deals with the handling of For Sale By Owner situations.

Mobile Homes. Mobile homes are a special case of the For Sale By Owner listing opportunity. In many states, real estate salespeople are allowed to handle the sale of mobile homes installed on rental spaces. In other states, real estate agents can sell only mobile homes with lots. Whatever your state restrictions, mobile homes make excellent listings. Many real estate professionals specialize in mobile home listings and sales.

Besides the classified For Sale ads, simply driving through mobile home parks will provide additional listing sources. Possibly because mobile home sales are not actively pursued by many real estate salespeople, there seems to be a far greater percentage of mobile homes For Sale By Owner than with conventional homes.

Mobile home park living in many ways is like small town life of years ago. Because of the large number of retired people and common social and recreational areas, people know each other and what is happening. Leads can be found simply by asking people in the clubhouse, laundry room or other facilities if they know of anyone who might be interested in selling their mobile home. Retired people will often be eager to talk to you.

It is comparatively easy to build up sources of information in a mobile home park. As a matter of fact, a mobile home park can make an excellent farm for your listing. In addition to simply asking, check the bulletin boards that are probably located in the recreation building or laundry facilities.

Mobile home equipment dealers often have bulletin boards where owners list their coaches for sale, lease, or lease option. While the dollar amount of mobile home sales averages less than other housing, mobile home sales generally are easier to make and in many areas are less affected by recessionary periods.

Special Newspapers. People who canvass newspapers often fail to consider that there are other papers besides the large daily ones. There are religious and ethnic newspapers in English as well as in foreign languages. Most areas have papers aimed at a particular professional, economic or special interest market.

Probably the best papers to check are the legal newspapers. These indicate problems such as creditor actions, bankruptcy notices, divorces, foreclosures, probates, etc. If your area has such a newspaper, it can be a gold mine of referrals.

Dodge Reports. Mention should be made of one professional paper of exceptional interest. *Dodge Construction News*, published by McGraw-Hill Information Systems Company, provides information on construction projects out for bid, contract awards and building permits, as well as classified ads for buildings and space for sale and for lease. A firm having new facilities built often wants to sell surplus facilities.

The reports also provide lien information. Liens indicate builder or owner financial problems which could mean a sale of real property.

THE LEGAL WORLD

Besides creditor action, the law reaches into every aspect of our lives, especially where property is concerned. If you have the constitution to deal with the tragedy and loss that legal action often brings, you have an opportunity to help solve problems and give help where it is badly needed. To get started, you must learn where to look and how to approach the listing leads you find.

Probate. Probate is the legal procedure for handling the estate of a deceased person. The debts of the deceased are paid, and the balance of the estate is then distributed to the heirs or beneficiaries.

Sometimes property must be sold during probate to pay bills, taxes and probate costs. A sale of property may also be required when the deceased leaves cash to beneficiaries and the estate has insufficient cash to carry out those directions.

Heirs who live out of the area are likely to want to sell the property they inherit. For an initial contact, I recommend a phone call in which you offer to perform a competitive market analysis. You can be sure that the heirs will be anxious to learn what the property they are to receive is worth.

Probate information is of public record and available at your county courthouse.

Arrests, Convictions and Acquittals. Criminal action can mean listings for a number of reasons. Money could be needed for criminal defense or to support the family. Very often, even when a person has been acquitted of a crime, that person or the family will desire to leave the area where the reputation has been compromised.

I recommend that these leads be handled with a canvass that makes no mention of the problems of the owners or their families:

"Mr. Gordon, I am Jane Goodman from Cosmos Realty. We recently sold the home at 4712 West Willow on the next block. We have had a great deal of interest in this area. I would be happy to give you, without obligation, a competitive market analysis that shows what you can expect to realize should you wish to place your home on the market."

Don't ask if he is interested in selling: Mr. Gordon will tell you if he isn't, even without being asked. On the other hand, he might deny that he is contemplating a sale, and you will have no way to continue the conversation. Instead, continue with questions such as:

"How many bedrooms do you have, Mr. Gordon?"

"Do you have two full baths?"

If Mr. Gordon answers these questions you can be sure that he has at the very least been considering selling. Then continue:

"Would it be all right if I came in to evaluate your home?"

Heading Off Foreclosures. Notices of foreclosure can be found in newspapers, legal newspapers, and on courthouse and county clerk's office bulletin boards. Mortgage foreclosures result when owners are unable to meet their financial obligations. All too often the owners refuse to believe that they can really lose their homes. They wait too long and lose a lifetime of savings because they grasp at straws while ignoring reality.

Owners of foreclosed properties usually lose everything. Your job is to show them that they may be able to sell before foreclosure is completed, thereby saving not only some of their equity, but some of their credit standing and pride, as well. Real estate ethics prohibit scare tactics, but if explaining the stark realities of a completed foreclosure is a scare tactic, I advise you to scare. You must dispel the head-in-the-sand attitude that everything will somehow work out all right. If you allow the owner to remain in a rosy fantasyland, you are doing a disservice.

Contact owners early enough in the foreclosure process to allow for a sale at near-market value. If time is short, owners will have to sell at bargain rates to ensure a quick sale. Some brokers set up auction sales before foreclosure is complete. This appeals to owners who know they must sell within a specific period of time. Having an auction of several properties at the same time gives you an especially strong listing appeal.

"Foreclosure Saviors." Some unethical real estate salespeople who call themselves "foreclosure saviors" offer to advance the owner funds to stop the foreclosure and take a second mortgage for their advance. What usually happens is that they end up doing the foreclosing themselves, taking over the owner's equity for the modest sum that they advanced.

Other "saviors" take a quitclaim deed from the owners and lease the home back to them under a rental agreement. The rental agreement allows the former owners an option to buy back their property if they pay the sum advanced plus interest by a specified date. It sounds like the answer to the homeowner's prayers, but seldom is. The agreement usually states that the option will be lost if the renter is more than a stated number of days late with any rental payment. Since the rental payments are higher than the mortgage payments the owners could not manage, the "savior" ends up owning the house for a small advance.

Sharp practices like this cannot be condoned. Your competition for foreclosure listings will be operators of this sort. Point out to owners that these operators are not out to help them, but to help themselves to their home equity. Through your better business bureau or district attorney's office you may be able to get names of people who lost their homes to these operators. Having an owner make a call to one of these people can be very effective. Ordinarily you should avoid speaking ill of competitors, but I strongly believe you have a positive duty to warn owners about unethical operators. You cannot allow an owner to be bilked when you could have alerted the owner.

Checking Liens. Just the fact that a property is in foreclosure does not make it a good listing. Often neglect, loans, liens or overvaluation have piled up more liabilities than a property is worth. Salespeople who specialize in foreclosure property have preliminary title reports prepared as soon as they get such listings. These reveal all recorded liens. Often what an owner says is against a property and what actually is against it are very different.

Even in such cases, you may be able to turn the property into a good listing. Junior lienholders can often be convinced to take less than their lien amounts. This is especially true when foreclosure is by the senior lienholder. If the holder of the first mortgage forecloses, all these junior lienholders end up with nothing. Most people are realistic enough to take less rather than nothing.

Suppose a property can be readily sold for $130,000 and the first mortgagee is foreclosing on a $90,000 first mortgage. Assume the owners also have a $100,000 judgment against them because of an automobile accident. The judgment would also be a lien against the real estate. The holder of this judgment will probably agree to accept the net proceeds of the sale or even less if the owners seem otherwise unlikely to pay the full amount. The owners benefit by the removal of the judgment without resorting to bankruptcy, and the judgment holder gets something rather than nothing.

This Power approach will make sense to a sophisticated creditor.

Evictions. The eviction notices you find indicated in the court calendar point to properties where owners have problems. You can offer a solution: sale of the property. An owner who had no interest in selling when there were few problems may quickly change when he or she experiences the lost rent, aggravation and cost that go with tenant eviction. This is especially true when single-family homes are involved. Usually such housing is owned by people who are not used to dealing with the legal and emotional problems eviction brings with it. Chances are they purchased a new home and decided to rent their old home, expecting a trouble-free income. They got more than they bargained for.

When an owner lives out of town, a phone call could be very productive. It is all right to live some distance from your income property when you have no problems, but when trouble comes the absentee owner feels especially helpless.

Personal Property Repossessions. Repossessions are an indication of serious financial difficulty. Debtors may be still making house payments while losing their car, furniture, boat and other property. Easy personal credit has gotten even people with excellent incomes into serious trouble. When debt piles up, even slight fluctuations in income lead to default. People having these problems are logical candidates for a home sale. Such a decision can solve their financial problems and allow them a chance to start over, clear of personal debt.

In some areas repossession actions are posted on courthouse bulletin boards. Other sources include special newspapers of legal notices and local courthouse records.

Bankruptcies. People who go bankrupt absolve themselves of their unsecured debts. Because of state laws, they generally are able to keep their homes.

The social stigma of bankruptcy often drives the affected parties to leave the area in order to start fresh somewhere else. By providing a competitive market analysis, you can show owners how the money from a sale can give them a stake with which to start rebuilding their lives.

When the reason for bankruptcy is a business loss, the bankrupt party often wants to return to the same business. The sale of a home could provide the bankrupt with the capital to try again. Many very successful business people have overcome bankruptcy to finally triumph.

You can find bankruptcy information in legal newspapers and courthouses. Bankrupts should be approached with the same tact you use when working from death notices or arrests, convictions or acquittals.

Attorneys. Attorneys are an excellent source of listings. They frequently have clients who have money problems, sometimes caused by the attorney's fee. By supplying a competitive market analysis to these clients, you show them a way to raise substantial cash. This may be needed in divorce cases, partnership dissolutions, probate and other legal activities.

In many states, attorneys handle title opinions and real estate closings. Buyers and sellers who don't have regular attorneys may ask the real estate salesperson for recommendations. One broker I know recommends several competent attorneys whose offices also happen to handle quite a few probate cases. The broker seems to get most of the probate listings from those offices.

Police. Police in a community know what is happening. Aside from criminal and domestic problems, they talk to many people each day. Friends on the local police force can provide you with excellent leads and strong referrals.

THE WORLD OF FINANCE

Real estate is inseparable from financial institutions and procedures. Knowing your way around the financial world and the local people who influence it should be a top priority in your efforts to develop ongoing sources of listing leads.

This section gives you tips on where to start and how to follow through.

Banks and S & Ls. Few banks and savings and loan institutions really want to foreclose: they want loans kept current or else paid off. Because of this attitude, lending institutions can be an excellent source of listings. Some lenders will actually suggest that you contact delinquent owners before foreclosure starts. I know of several cases where small lenders held off foreclosure because the property was listed for sale at a realistic price. Larger lenders are more likely to "go by the book" and foreclose according to their set schedules.

When banks and other lenders do foreclose, they have property to convert to cash as quickly as possible. If you can provide the complete services needed to protect the property, put it in salable condition and sell it, you can develop a reputation that brings in lenders as clients. The trick is to get your first foreclosure resale and handle it successfully.

I suggest starting where you do your own banking. Make a lunch appointment with the bank officer who handles foreclosures. Tell him or her what you have in mind, mentioning along the way the substantial trust account your office maintains with his or her bank. While reducing fees is generally not recommended, in this case a special deal may be needed to get you the chance to show what you can do.

Once the listing is obtained, your task is to protect, repair, and sell the property as quickly as possible. When property is being foreclosed, owners usually neglect maintenance, and may leave it unprotected and vulnerable to vandalism. Unless lenders have in-house departments able to handle all these details, they must deal with a broker who can meet their special needs.

Trust Departments. Trust departments of banks also get real estate they must sell. Since trust officers prefer to deal with cash and securities, they will usually sell any real property included in a trust. Trust officers are people whose acquaintance pays dividends.

Finance Companies. Managers of small loan firms also make excellent contacts. If a homeowner is having difficulty paying a loan on personal property, a home sale could mean the cash to liquidate the loan. Most lenders strongly prefer cash rather than title to the loan security. A home sale could allow repayment of the loan. Loan officers won't give you details of a borrower's troubles as this is generally regarded as confidential. They might suggest, however, that certain families could be considering selling their homes.

Installment Dealers. Home improvement firms and even some home furnishing and carpet dealers take second mortgages to secure their notes. Foreclosures by such firms are common because they frequently overburden an owner. While the ethics of these firms may be questionable, they are usually operating inside the law. By selling these firms on your services, you can obtain a continuing source of listings. A strong point to push in obtaining these listings is your ability to arrange and supervise the cleaning and renovation necessary to maximize the seller's profit.

Personnel Offices. I know a real estate salesman who tries to take at least one personnel officer from a major area employer to lunch every week. He believes that the few dollars he spends for lunch have resulted in leads that brought in thousands of dollars in commissions.

Personnel offices can tell you who is being transferred to and from the area, who has had a promotion, who has been terminated, and who is retiring. All these leads can result in listings as well as sale possibilities.

Since you are providing a needed service, many personnel officers will be very cooperative. But don't expect to receive advance notice of decisions before the parties involved are told.

Pre-Retirement Programs. Some large businesses have pre-retirement programs for their employees. You can establish a good relationship with the personnel office by preparing a presentation as part of such programs. Your presentation can help you make excellent listings contacts, but should give no hint that this is part of your purpose. Make the presentation honest and straightforward, giving practical advice of special interest to retirees, such as:

1. The pros and cons of relocation.

2. The costs of selling a home.

3. Understanding owner financing and the annuity aspects of various types of sales.

4. Protect yourself—How to guard against shady operators who prey on retirees, trying to either "steal" their homes or sell them near-worthless property.

Firms That Buy Employee Homes. Many firms have encountered problems in convincing employees to transfer to another locality, even though the transfer means a promotion. A major reason has been the problems owners have encountered in selling their homes, and the high costs of buying new ones. Because of these problems, many large firms now agree to buy an employee's home if he or she cannot sell it. In some cases they also finance a new home purchase at below-market rates.

The personnel officers of firms that buy employee homes are worth particular attention. You can help them by selling employees' homes so the company need not purchase them. A private sale will often net the employee more than a sale at the company's price.

Once you show these firms that you are interested in helping them and are competent, you have a good chance of obtaining listings on the homes they purchase.

THE PUBLIC EYE

Not all your contacts have to be one-on-one relationships. Using various ways to earn public recognition will make you familiar to potential clients who have never met you in person. There are many ways to get your name and face before the public. All of them pay large dividends for careful preparation and hard work.

Public Speaking. Service clubs such as Rotary, Lions, Kiwanis, Optimists International, Soroptimists and Exchange Club, as well as church men's groups, are always looking for speakers. I suggest that you prepare a 20-minute talk on a real estate topic that interests you and will interest your audience. For example,

1. Reduce Your Taxes Through Real Estate

2. What the New Tax Laws Mean to Property Owners

3. The Crystal Ball—Our Real Estate Market in the Coming Months

4. High-Leverage Investment Techniques

Generally, your audience will consist of property owners with good present or future incomes. Selling yourself as a professional can go a long way toward obtaining future listings. When a person you are contacting for a listing remembers that you spoke to her at Soroptomists last month, she sees you as a competent professional rather than as a stranger knocking on her door.

Teaching. Community colleges and adult continuation schools that offer classes in real estate are always looking for knowledgeable instructors. Besides gratifying your ego, teaching gives you a special relationship with your students, and the inside track on their future business.

Press Releases. Press releases keep your contacts aware that you are a real estate professional and welcome their help. They also provide recognition for yourself and your firm, so initial contacts become more than just cold calls.

Your local newspaper will generally print press releases if your firm is an advertiser. Real estate sections of most newspapers are made up primarily of press releases and advertisements.

Licensees starting work with a new firm should submit press releases with a glossy black-and-white photograph. While no substitute for personal contact, press releases reach acquaintances you never even thought of.

Many offices are always giving salespeople titles—sales manager, assistant sales manager, manager of tract sales, manager of sales for a particular tract or area, director of residential sales, director of the commercial and investment division, and so on. When a salesperson is appointed to one of these positions, a press release with a photograph of the salesperson is submitted to the local papers.

The press release should be completely typed out in a professional manner. I suggest it be headed "Press Release —For Immediate Publication." Larger offices may find it worthwhile to have press release forms printed up. These might be headed *News From* [Office Name].

The release itself should have a short, catchy heading. Most papers will not rewrite the release, so if it is poorly written it won't be published. Smaller newspapers are more likely to print your releases, and the more you advertise the more likely that all of it will be published.

LISTENING TO THE PEOPLE YOU KNOW

Listening is an overlooked source of listings, since few of us really listen to what is being said. Most of us want to tell rather than listen. It is easy to get enamored by our own voices. It's hard to get used to, but you will find that "small talk" can be productive when you ask questions and probe for information, letting the other person be the center of the conversation.

People we talk to in our daily lives often drop clues to listing opportunities. Gossip concerns itself with success, failure or the problems of others, all of which may involve good reasons to sell property. Here are some places where it pays to start listening, and ways to develop your information network.

The Recruiting and Care of Bird Dogs. The term "bird dog" is not derogatory. A bird dog is simply someone who points the way to an opportunity by pointing out useful facts and situations.

The best bird dogs don't work for personal reward. They are simply people who like you and want to help you succeed. A friend of mine has his mother as a full-time bird dog. She drops in or calls him every day, bawling him out about his clothes, grooming, weight or messy office. She also provides quality leads. Incidentally, he is in his mid-50s.

The secret of cultivating referrals and bird dogs is to let people know that you sincerely want their help. Make sure they know exactly what type of information and/or referrals you want.

A skilled hunter pats a dog on the head for a job well done. You, too, must find ways to show appreciation if you expect the help to continue. Let people know the results of their leads. A salesperson who fails to do this will soon find his sources drying up. A birthday and/or Christmas gift also helps. Quality chocolates or "top shelf" liquor are appreciated. Even more meaningful are gifts that relate to a person's special interests—a rare coin for a coin collector, a fine putter for a golfer, a quality fishing rod for a person who likes to fish. To be most effective, give something your helpers desire but would not ordinarily buy for themselves. Taking helpers and their spouses out to dinner at a fine restaurant is another way of showing your appreciation.

Splitting commissions with unlicensed persons is illegal. In many states, paying a referral fee is legal and many real estate people pay their sources. I personally do not feel that cash payments are necessary or proper.

Referrals. Referrals are extremely strong leads. When owners contact you on the advice of a mutual friend or business acquaintance, your job is half accomplished. The owners contacted you because they have confidence in your mutual friend or acquaintance who, in turn, has indicated trust in you. When you contact a prospect at the request of a mutual friend or acquaintance, you still have a strong advantage. You have been asked to help a friend, not make a cold contact.

The relationship between the owners and the person who referred you is, of course, very important. The closer the owners are to that person, the stronger will be your position.

Friends. Your friends must not only know you are in the real estate business, they must also know you want their help. Bumper stickers such as "Have You Hugged Your Realtor Today" and magnetic car signs constantly remind your friends that you are in the real estate business as well as spread the word outside your circle. Wearing your Realtor ® pin or firm emblem also serves as a reminder. Many firms have their salespeople wear distinctive shirts or jackets.

Strive to increase your circle of friends. Activity in special interest groups can be very valuable. If you are interested in investment property listings, consider becoming active in one of the many apartment owner organizations.

If you went to school in your area, consider your friends of long ago. Look through your old high school yearbook. You will recall former close friends who you probably haven't thought of in years. These friendships can be renewed with a call, visit or an invitation.

Your Neighbors. Be sure your own neighbors know that you are in the real estate business and are interested in serving them. Another broker's sign on a house in your neighborhood is a confession of failure. Worse yet is having another broker's For Sale sign on the building that contains your office.

When you move into a neighborhood, or are just starting in real estate, introduce yourself to each neighbor for at least a block around. Learn their names and addresses and get to know them by their first names. Make sure they all know that you are in the real estate business. You can expand this island of influence several blocks by letters. Make your own neighborhood part of your farm.

Learn to walk. Stop and say a few words with neighbors who are washing their cars or working on their lawns. Tell your neighbors about sales in the area. People are always interested in what their homes are worth. Make sure they all know you are in the business and would like to serve them.

People don't like to work with losers, so act confident and successful. It's just basic role-playing, but you will do much better if people think you are successful. You want people to know you want their business and their help, but you don't want them to think you need their business to survive.

Previous Buyers. By regular contacts you can turn previous buyers into friends. Birthday, anniversary and Christmas cards, along with a personal note, can remind them of your relationship. One salesman sends a telegram to newborn children of his past customers which says "Congratulations (child's name) for choosing two swell parents like Jim and Kathy."

Cards and letters won't do it on their own. You also need several phone contacts each year. I know real estate people who have one large party each year, usually around Christmas, to which they invite former buyers and people who help them in various ways to obtain listings and sales.

Customers of salespeople who are no longer with your office can become excellent sources of listings. The relationship which was built up in making a sale, even though it was by another salesperson, can be revived. A phone call such as the following would be a good start:

"Mr. Smith, I am Craig Randall with Park Realty. When you purchased your home seven years ago through our firm, I bet you never thought it would be worth its present value?"

You want to point out what your firm did for them. Take some credit for their good fortune.

"I am trying to help a young couple with a seven-year-old daughter who are looking for a home in your area. They would very much like their daughter to attend Hoover School."

Asking help for a specific buyer rather than buyers in general is a Power approach. People seldom refuse their cooperation when asked to help specific individuals.

"Do you know anyone in your area who might consider selling their home? Is there anyone who has had a change in family size because of marriage, divorce, death, birth or graduation?"

Follow up this call with a personal note, with your card enclosed, thanking the person for his or her help. Chances are the homeowners are very glad that they purchased their home through your office. What you are doing is rediscovering and renewing this good will. It's foolish to let it go to waste.

Neighborhood Ears. If you make it a point to pay attention to who knows what in your own neighborhood, you'll never run short of good leads. Here are some people and places to keep in touch with. Once you get in the habit of seeing your own area as a prime hunting ground, you'll think of dozens more.

Religious Leaders. Ministers, priests and rabbis know what is happening. Their knowledge of the personal plans and problems of their congregations can be very valuable. Their referrals carry a great deal of weight because they are usually highly respected and trusted individuals.

Start with your own religious leader. Get involved in your church organizations and make sure your religious leader knows you are in real estate and are interested in sale and purchase possibilities.

When you find a house for a family that wanted to be close to a church of a particular denomination or in a particular parish, contact the leader of that church. Ask him or her to welcome the new family, and you have begun an excellent relationship.

Barbers and Beauticians. People talk to their barbers and beauticians, who become warehouses of information. While they are working on your hair, try to tap this source —who is planning retirement to another area, moving up in housing or planning to sell for any other reason?

Bartenders. People like to tell their troubles to bartenders. They can be an exceptional source of leads. If you specialize in this source, however, your liver may give out before the rest of your body is ready for retirement.

ADDITIONAL SOURCES

There are many opportunities for listings besides newspapers and legal or financial sources. The following are just the surface of the listing opportunities all around you every day.

Expired Listings. Expired listings usually mean highly motivated sellers, but to reap their potential rewards, you must be able to overcome the owners' suspicious attitude brought on by the broken promises of others.

The best way to show that you are on the seller's side is to offer to analyze why the property didn't sell. This can be brought up during the first phone contact:

> "I believe I will be able to tell you why your home has not as yet sold. Would it be all right if I stopped by to discuss the problems with you and Mr. Jones at seven this evening?"

Another approach uses your office's neighborhood experience as an ice breaker:

> "Our office has just sold the Kilbourns' home on your block as well as several other homes in your area. I believe I will be able . . ."

Chances are the house didn't sell because the original lister took it with an unrealistic price and/or noncompetitive terms. Other possibilities include the condition of the premises or the advertising and sales approach of the previous listing office.

When you meet with the owner, you should have a pretty good idea of the property's value. If the owner appears receptive to the price you suggest, go for the listing.

Normally, an owner who has been disappointed by a previous agent's results will not come around that easily. To give your opinions more weight, try the Power approach of bringing in your entire office sales staff to view the property. This can be done before or after a regular sales meeting. Now you have an analysis that represents the consensus of a whole group of real estate experts. The consensus report will bear much more weight than an individual viewpoint, especially since the property did not sell.

The report should be in writing, presented in a folder similar to the competitive market analysis discussed in Chapter 4. If the group consensus calls for a price reduction, a competitive market analysis should be included in the report. Don't recommend a price cut unless the facts show that the property was overpriced or that the owner *must* have a quick sale.

Prospective Buyers. When you qualify prospective buyers, you may find that they have to become sellers before they can buy. If their property has not yet been listed, change the direction of your efforts from a sale to a listing.

When you have buyers who must sell before they can buy a specific property, try for an offer contingent upon the sale of their home within a stated time limit. Present the offer to the owners along with a copy of the signed listing to show that your buyer is serious. If the home of the buyer is more salable than the home they are buying, then the contingent offer is likely to be accepted. Builders with a number of homes to sell are especially likely to accept such a contingent offer.

Rejected Property. When sale prospects mention that they looked at another property, ask them about it: why didn't they buy it? who was trying to sell it? If the property was not with a broker, it could make an excellent opportunity for you. Your knowledge of why one prospect did not buy gives you ammunition that other salespeople do not have. You can explain the problem and offer a solution. If the prospects were turned off by the high price, down payment, or the other conditions, you have an opening for explaining alternative financing techniques.

Pre-1981 Investment Property Buyers. People who purchased improved income or investment property prior to 1981 are logical prospects for listings and sales. These buyers are probably depreciating the improvements on their property over a 25- to 50-year period. A sale and a new purchase now could be extremely advantageous to them even if their profit is subject to capital gains tax. By utilizing their proceeds and buying a similar property, they can now depreciate the improvements over 15 years. In addition, they are allowed to take 175 percent declining balance depreciation, giving even greater benefits during the early years of ownership.

Don't be afraid to get the owner's accountant involved in the decision to list. You will find that most accountants will recommend a sale and purchase for people in upper tax brackets.

Architects and Designers. Architects and designers usually start designing new facilities and homes long before their clients have placed their property on the market. People having property built for them know that the design, approval and construction process takes time.

A working relationship with architects and designers can be mutually beneficial. When you sell a lot to a buyer who intends to build on it rather than hold it as an investment, you can recommend a competent architect or designer. Architects and designers can in turn refer to you owners who plan to sell their present property when their new homes are ready.

Builders. Builders are an excellent source of listings. The most obvious listings are the homes the builder produces for resale. Some brokers have built up a relationship with particular builders that spans many years, and they get all that builder's listings. Many brokers have grown with the builders they work with. They may have started selling a few homes on scattered lots but now handle whole subdivisions for that builder.

In addition to their own sale inventory, builders often have prospects who can't become buyers until they sell their present homes. By taking that listing you benefit the builder and yourself. Some brokers work with builders in setting up trade-in plans where the real estate agent evaluates and sells the trade-in.

Builders do not easily give out listings. You must first convince them that you can do what the builders cannot do for themselves. Then you have to show how you offer more benefits than other agents.

The strongest sales approach is success with one builder. If you dispose of inventory for a builder while other builders' sales are in a slump, contact the other builders and tell them about it. Builders are businessmen: nothing impresses them more than demonstrated success.

Subdividing. If you are competent in the subdivision and/or condominium conversion processes, you will obtain long-term listings on many properties, plus a fee for your services. In approaching owners of land ripe for subdivision, or owners of potential condominium buildings, offer to prepare a proposal covering all costs and estimated sales prices. You may want to include proposals on how to finance the subdivision or conversion expenses.

If you like paperwork and getting involved in small details, condominium conversions might well suit your needs. This specialized ability can give you considerable leverage in obtaining large numbers of listings. Land subdivisions require either an engineering background or a close working relationship with civil engineers.

Some offices actively subdivide their own land, thus providing an inventory of lots as well as a source of new home listings. Brokers will often agree to subordinate the land if the builder agrees to begin construction at once and to give the broker exclusive-right-to-sell listings.

Subordination means that the seller will take back a second mortgage for the land. The first mortgage goes to the construction lender. This means that the lot seller could lose his or her interest in the lot without compensation should the construction lender foreclose.

While there are risks, many subdividers are willing to subordinate in order to get construction activity started, as this helps sell the remaining lots and brings in listings. Builders like these arrangements since they don't have to tie up capital in the land.

Property Management. Besides earning fees for you, property management serves as an excellent source of sale listings.

Managing property gives you the chance to earn the owner's trust and respect. If you understand the owner's needs you can point out the advantages of selling or exchanging property. If an owner has fully depreciated real estate and is in a high tax bracket, you might recommend to the owner and his or her accountant that the property be sold and capital gains taxes paid. Reinvesting the proceeds in another property then provides for rapid depreciation. When property has appreciated a great deal, the simple act of presenting a competitive market analysis can result in a listing.

Even if you don't manage property yourself, you can still use most of these techniques. Simply keep in close contact with the property management division within your office. It will supply you with a steady source of listings, as well as transferring to you some of the respect your firm has earned by its faithful service to property owners.

Condominium Associations. Condominium associations are usually in need of professional help. Many try at first to operate with association members, then give up and hire a professional manager who handles financial planning, fee assessment, record keeping, insurance coverage, supervision of maintenance and repairs, and enforcement of condominium regulations.

Many real estate agents have discovered that there is "gold in them thar condominiums," not so much from their fees as from business generated through member contacts. The manager-broker can expect to represent most of the owners when they sublease or sell.

I know a broker who bid to perform management duties for a large resort-area condominium association. He offered to provide an agent to handle condominium association business for 40 hours every week without cost to the association. The owners quickly accepted his proposal, and agreed to process all rentals through his office at an agreed fee. He has listed over 150 condos for sale in the three years he has handled the complex, and collected fees on countless rentals. The free office the association provided also serves as his firm's general business office.

If you are interested in condominium management, I suggest you obtain a copy of *Condominium Management* by Jack R. Holeman (Prentice-Hall, 1980). The Institute of Real Estate Management publishes *The Condominium Community: a Guide for Owners, Boards and Managers* and *Expense Analysis: Condominiums, Cooperatives and PUD's*. Order these from the Institute of Real Estate Management of the National Association of Realtors®, 430 N. Michigan Avenue, Chicago, Illinois 60611.

Movers. Moving and storage firms can help you just as you can help them. Many people contact movers for an estimate as soon as they contemplate moving. Whether it's a job offer in another city, a promotion, or retirement, knowing what homeowners are thinking as soon as the mover does can keep you a big step ahead of the competition.

For their part, movers want to know when an offer has been accepted on a house, especially when the seller will be leaving the area. Mutual interests make practical a close relationship with a mover. Some salespeople exchange information with a large moving firm several times each week.

SPECIALIZE

I have suggested far more listing sources than anyone can ever make good use of. Don't try to work them all—it isn't possible. I recommend trying various sources and settling on the ones you feel comfortable working with.

Specializing can be handled so that every transaction leads to more listings and sales. One saleswoman makes her specialization in horse-related properties work this way. She gets leads from the horse clubs and associations she belongs to, and also from every sale and listing she obtains. Horse owners associate with other horse owners, so she questions each buyer and seller to find out about friends who have specific needs such as larger properties to hold more horses, or smaller properties to hold a reduced number of animals. The agent keeps card files of several thousand horse owners from her contacts. Besides personal contacts she canvasses her entire file with mailings several times each year.

Just as you should consider specialization in sales activity, specialization in listing sources will make your efforts pay off. Specialization will enable you to develop a smooth professional approach which will give you greater confidence. Confidence will, in turn, motivate you for greater success.

3

Getting Leads and Getting In

Using the sources and techniques from Chapter 2 will give you all the listing possibilities you can handle. Possibilities, however, must become solid leads before you can move to a listing presentation. However you find your sources, the time comes to start knocking on doors for appointments with the owners. This chapter details proven techniques for successful canvassing, and strategies for getting you over the threshhold.

DOOR-TO-DOOR CANVASSING

In a door-to-door real estate canvass you are not trying to sell a product. Rather you are seeking and giving information. The canvass allows you to find not only the real estate needs of a household, but the needs of neighbors and friends, as well.

Most real estate salespeople do not actively canvass for listings. That may be why most real estate salespeople do not succeed. Canvassing and success are directly related. Some salespeople claim that door-to-door solicitation is unprofessional—that cold-canvassing is undignified and harmful to real estate's public image.

I see this reasoning as an excuse that covers up two real reasons for shying away from canvassing. First, canvassing is work, and work doesn't fit the image of what some salespeople think they should be doing. In their minds, they belong in nice cars showing nice homes to nice people. Ringing doorbells isn't part of their picture of success.

The second real reason is fear. When I first started selling Watkins Products door to door, I had to force myself to ring a doorbell. When I did ring it, I prayed that no one would answer it. I would dream up excuses not to ring particular doorbells and reasons why I shouldn't be doing this and why I should quit for the day. From discussions with other salespeople engaged in door-to-door selling, I found that my reactions were not unusual.

Nobody likes rejection: it's hard to take. During my days with Watkins Products, we were constantly getting new hirees who would last only a day or two. After a month of sales, I was second in seniority in a crew of six salespeople.

My crew leader used to say, "What's the worst thing that can happen to you? A little verbal abuse?" On the positive side was an order and success. The benefits far outweighed the negative aspects of canvassing. As I started seeing improvements in my results, my feelings of apprehension over ringing doorbells changed. Ringing a doorbell became a challenge, a chance for success, not a possibility of failure.

One week of door-to-door solicitation, I believe, can provide you with more sales experience than six months of conventional real estate sales situations. Door-to-door canvassing gives you personal confidence in dealing with a wide variety of people. It provides you the opportunity to experiment and develop effective presentations you are comfortable with.

Using Canned Presentations. I was lucky when I learned to canvass. My crew leader took me out with him for half a day, so I learned how he used a "canned" presentation with several alternate closings. I got a chance to see how well the approach worked. I quickly realized the importance of having the proper words ready, and became a firm believer in canned presentations.

A canned presentation is a carefully planned presentation repeated word for word. Not that every presentation is exactly the same. They vary with products, customer interest, and objections. I used a canned introduction, canned answers to similar objections, canned benefits in selling products, and canned closings.

National organizations selling everything from computers to insurance realize that canned presentations sell. Even though a salesperson knows the product, an ad-libbed presentation is unlikely to cover all the important benefits in the most attractive terms, or to lead to an effective closing at the right time.

Canned presentations also provide a basic approach that you can refine and improve with experience. When I lost a sale, I would try to analyze why and work on my presentation to convey desirable images. Finally I developed a smooth method for answering questions and handling objections. My sales increased until I was the top producer in my crew. By consistent use of canned presentations, I was able to learn from my failures.

Using Directories. Your door-to-door canvassing doesn't have to be completely cold. Street directories provide the names of the residents at each address, and some include family size and even occupations. By copying the appropriate pages of the directory, you have a way to address people by name. Use the owner's name as often as you can. People like to be called by name. If you are unsure of the pronunciation ask the person, "Mr. Garczynski, is my pronunciation correct?" People are turned off when their names are mispronounced.

Using Your Image. When you ring a doorbell, step back several steps or you may appear menacing. The least threatening image is achieved by looking away from the door so you present a profile, and smiling.

You may be observed through peepholes, so a neat appearance is very important. A briefcase can be menacing, so use a clipboard, file folder or notebook. Women have a distinct advantage over men in cold solicitations since people feel less threatened by a woman and are more likely to invite a woman into their homes.

Using Giveaways. Many salespeople like to start a presentation by giving something away—a pen, ruler, calendar, horoscope or newsletter. If the owner has a newspaper on the lawn, you can pick it up to give to him or her. Acceptance of a freebie forces a thank-you and an obligation to listen, although every owner may not understand this obligation. I personally don't find giveaways necessary, but many salespeople feel they make excellent openers.

Canvassing Where You've Sold. Sales of your office listings indicate success. When your Sold sign goes up, you have a temporary edge over every other office for getting more listings in the area. To take advantage of this windfall, canvass at least one block around each Sold sign with your office's name on it, whether or not your office actually made the sale. If it was your listing, your office was responsible for it.

When you talk to homeowners near the sold property, bring them the news at once:

> "Good afternoon, Mrs. Schmidt. I am Carl Thompson from Uptown Realty. We have just [or recently] sold the Kowalski home at 2911 Elm just down the block, the house with the large pine tree in the front yard. The new owners are Mr. and Mrs. Collins. He is an engineer and she teaches first grade at Sunnyside School. They have one daughter nine years old. I hope you will welcome them to your neighborhood."

People are curious about their new neighbors, so they will listen to what you have to say. Make the new neighbors sound as ideal as possible; people like to help nice people. A plea to welcome new neighbors will usually be well received. Continue with,

"As you undoubtedly realize, you live in a desirable neighborhood. In advertising the Kowalskis' home we were contacted by several other families whose needs we have been unable to meet. Right now I am looking for a home for a very fine family. He is an accountant who is being transferred here from Ohio. They have two sons, ages three and six. I need help in finding them a home. Do you know anyone in the area who is planning to move? Has anyone in the area recently had a change in family size because of marriage, divorce, birth or death? Has anyone recently retired?"

You have first demonstrated your competence, then you have given the owner information about a new neighbor, and now you are asking help for a particular need situation. This technique is very effective because you are there with positive news.

Since few salespeople bother to canvass, you can canvass the neighborhood of listings and sales of other salespeople in your office, but be sure to ask permission from the listing salespeople. The technique can be used with slight variations for sales your office made when the listing was with another office.

TELEPHONE CANVASSING

A telephone call is a long-distance knock on the door. A call is less effective than a personal contact because it is very difficult to build trust over the phone. Nevertheless, telephone canvassing can provide an excellent source of listing leads. In some areas door-to-door canvassing is not allowed. Telephone canvassing is the best available contact for these areas.

By using city directories it is possible to canvass specific areas by streets in much the same manner as you would with door-to-door canvassing. One advantage of telephone canvassing is that you can contact more owners per hour on the phone than by knocking on doors.

Check your local tax assessor's office for names and addresses of out-of-the-area owners. They tend to be much more willing to sell than local residents.

Telephone presentations, like personal contacts, should be planned in advance, preferably in writing. You can model your telephone approach on the door-to-door approaches previously covered. Don't vary too much from your planned approach. Keep in mind that your goal is to get through the front door.

If an owner indicates that he or she might consider selling, reinforce that option with an offer of a competitive market analysis:

"Before you make any decision, you should fully understand what you can reasonably expect to receive from a sale. Mr. Brown, I would like to perform a competitive market analysis on your home. By analyzing not only the sales price, but also the sales terms and the time it took to sell comparable properties, we can arrive at a realistic estimate of what your home will sell for. Many owners are pleasantly surprised to learn what their homes are worth. We perform this analysis at no cost or obligation to you. Would you and Mrs. Brown be home at 8 o'clock tonight so I can stop by and get the information needed for the analysis? Or would 8:30 be more convenient?"

When you get an appointment, end the conversation quickly. You are not going to get a listing over the phone, but you could give the owner an opportunity to change his or her mind about meeting with you.

MAIL SOLICITATIONS

While both personal and phone contacts are much more effective, you can productively use the mails for listings. Keep your mailed material simple, like this postcard:

**WANT TO KNOW WHAT YOUR HOME
IS WORTH IN TODAY'S MARKET?**

**Call JIM HILL at 978-4132
for a free evaluation**

COSMOS REALTY 2211 W. MAIN, BIGTOWN, CA 93701

Mail solicitations need an opener that grabs the reader:

**YOU DON'T MAKE A PROFIT UNTIL YOU SELL—
ARE YOU READY FOR A PROFIT?
WANT TO KNOW HOW MUCH MONEY
IS TIED UP IN YOUR HOUSE?**

The most productive group of recipients for direct mail solicitations are out-of-town owners. Indicate in large type that they should call you COLLECT. Saving the cost of a phone call for an owner could mean thousands of dollars in commissions.

Another approach that I strongly recommend is to indicate in your letter that you will be calling the owner. This forces an owner to think for a moment whether or not he or she wants to sell. When you call, your call will not be a normal cold canvass: the owner will be expecting your call.

Since you'll be investing considerable money in postage, consider spending a few cents more to have solicitation material printed with professional art work. The envelope and mailer information will still be the smallest part of your cost.

Letters which appear to be typed are more effective than printed ones. An automatic typewriter can provide these at reasonable cost. Here are some mail selling tips that are proven by over a dozen years of personal experience.

1. Don't use mass mailings until you test their effectiveness with a controlled mailing. Use different return phone numbers or box numbers on different versions of each mailing. Then you can determine the relative effectiveness of each by the number of replies you get at each box or phone number. One mail order firm recently got a brutal reminder of the importance of testing. They were sure they had a winner, so they bypassed the testing phase. They spent over $50,000 for their mailing and got total gross returns of slightly over $4,000.

2. Don't use a postage meter. A meter stamp makes your mailing piece look like junk mail. Use a first-class stamp, preferably a commemorative stamp. Tests have shown that envelopes with commemorative stamps are not only opened, they are usually opened first.

3. Hand-address your envelopes. Printed mailing labels or window envelopes look like junk mail.

4. Never address "To Occupant." This is an invitation to have the mailing piece thrown into the "round file" on the floor. Mr. and Mrs. Occupant don't give listings, but real people do.

5. Don't use your normal envelope with your logo. Use a plain envelope without a return address. This guarantees that your letter will be opened. Curiosity is a powerful force, and no one will throw out a letter when he or she has no idea what it contains. On the other hand, millions of pieces of obvious junk mail are trashed unopened.

6. Include a return envelope with a first-class mailing permit and a handy form for the owner to use for a reply.

FARMING

Farming is the cultivation of a specific area for listings by regular contacts with the owners.

Farm sizes vary, but I recommend no more than 500 homes. Two hundred to 400 are usually sufficient, but there will be times you will want to cover an entire 500-home subdivision.

Where to Farm. In choosing a farm area, consider your competition. Does the area have an active farmer now? Few real estate salespeople are willing to do the hard work farming requires, so you will easily find open areas. A one-day canvass will tell you if an area is actively farmed. There is no need to back off from competition, but if you have a choice, there is no point in farming an area where a salesperson has already developed an excellent relationship with the owners.

Newer tract areas of moderately-priced homes generally have a high percentage of first-time home buyers. Chances are that they have not developed much broker loyalty. Repeated contacts here can develop a strong relationship with such owners. Newer tract areas are desirable for several reasons:

1. Newer developments generally have a much higher turnover rate than older established areas.

2. In areas of more expensive homes, while commissions would be larger, owners have probably purchased several properties in the past and are likely to have developed broker loyalties.

3. People in moderately-priced homes are moving up economically and are more likely to move. They are also more likely to be transferred or change jobs. The turnover rate for more expensive homes is much lower than for more modestly priced homes. Generally, people in very expensive homes have arrived and are less likely to move. It takes as much time to service 300 homes having an average turnover of 14 percent as it does to service 300 homes with a 24 percent rate.

An ideal location for your farm is a tract where you handled the sales. Moving on to new tracts when a tract is sold out wastes many valuable contacts made not just in selling homes, but in working with a buyer on financing, construction problems, and other matters associated with the purchase. You should have developed a strong and positive personal relationship with hundreds of buyers. With this going for you, it won't take long to harvest the benefits of this farm.

Your farm area should be one in which you feel comfortable for both listings and sales. If you live in the area, you will have many ready-made contacts.

If you wish to increase the size of your farm, consider a contiguous area. It would be best if your areas are identifiable with names such as "Oakridge Estates" rather than "Between North Avenue and Clarke Street and between 45th Street and 50th Street."

Indexes of your farm owners with both street address and name will give you data for canvassing and answering owner calls. Having necessary information at your fingertips will impress owners with your professionalism and your close awareness of them and their property. Your data card on each property should include information about the owners and the property, plus a record of every contact made with your comments.

Harvesting Listings. Strive for at least one owner contact per month with every owner in your farm. Contacts can be person to person, by phone or by mail. Make your first contact a home solicitation. Should you encounter a hostile or abusive owner, don't bother making any more personal visits or phone calls with that owner unless you have a particular request for help. You should, of course, continue any area mailings to that owner.

Set aside definite blocks of time to work your farm with phone contacts, mail contacts and personal contacts. Without a definite schedule it will be too easy to put it off. Farming can be hard and tedious work and results take time. Many agents start farms but abandon them before they ever benefit from a crop of listings. They fail to realize that the longer they farm an area, the more productive it becomes.

Many real estate salespeople make very good livings on their farm listings alone. A farm area with 300 homes and an annual turnover of 22 percent would produce 66 home sales each year. A good farmer should get at least a third of these listings, or about two every month. In farming, success breeds success.   As you get more listings and sell them, people will consider you a person to contact for listings within the area.

If a resident of your farm area lists with another office despite your repeated contacts, don't be angry. Should you have contact with the owners, let them know they were smart to give an exclusive right-to-sell listing. If the property is not sold, move in when the listing expires. You have a second chance.

Tools. One excellent initial farming tool is a free horoscope.   The owners are asked to fill in their exact time of birth, plus wedding dates, names and dates of birth of children, jobs or professions, etc. This is a quick way to get extensive owner information for your files.

You should have a tickler file so that you can send out birthday and anniversary cards each week. Always write a personal note with the card and include a business card. Whenever you see any article in the newspapers about a resident of your farm, cut it out and mail it with a note, *Thought you would like this,* and your business card.

Consider volunteering to work on a major charity drive within your farm area, and taking part in local organizations and youth activities.   Such involvement gets you noticed in a favorable light.

Many salespeople use newsletters in their farm areas. You will see various newsletters advertised in real estate magazines.   Some salespeople use them as handouts as they canvass.   These commercial newsletters have your name printed on them but contain general information items: household hints and articles on the advantages of property ownership.   They can be used in canvassing, mailed, placed in giveaway racks at markets and motels, or given away at open houses.

If you are working a homogeneous area such as a retirement community, a condominium complex or other developments with a separate identity, your own newsletter can be much more effective than one you purchase. The local newsletter can include social events, youth activities, birthdays, anniversaries, hospitalizations, births, deaths and accomplish-

ments of local residents. It should also remind residents of
your value to them by showing whose property you have sold
to whom in the past month.

Much of the newsletter work can be done by volunteer
residents in your area, so your costs are limited to putting the
material together and printing. Such a newsletter is not
treated as junk literature. It is read regularly and keeps your
name before many people.

One salesperson I know has his newsletter professionally
printed and sells back-page ads which pay for the preparation
and distribution.

GETTING IN

You can't get a listing until you get through the front door.
Your first goal is to get in so you can talk to the owners.
The reason that many owners resist talking to real estate
agents is that they are afraid they will be talked into giving a
listing. They would like to complete the sale without an
agent so they can keep the real estate commission for themselves. It is up to you to prove that the advantages claimed
for For Sale By Owner efforts are not real. To prove the
falsity of such beliefs, however, you must first create a
chance to talk to the owners.

Never try to gain access to an owner's home by sub-
terfuge. This isn't necessary or ethical. You can't expect an
owner to develop a relationship of trust with you when your
relationship starts with deceit. Always indicate you are a real
estate agent; you are not a buyer, an inspector or anything
else.

Follow the golden rule in your solicitations. You are
not after a single listing or sale; you are building a career on
continuing sales and listings. Be honest in what you say and
be sure you have fully disclosed to owners what they should
know in order to make informed decisions. I have attended
seminars on real estate listings where fraud was actually
recommended.

One of the most unethical and self-destructive canvassing tactics is the use of race to scare owners into thinking

property values are being eroded by an influx of minorities. Besides violating the Realtors® Code of Ethics, such practices are punishable federal offenses.

The sad thing about dishonest approaches is that they are so unnecessary. Any salesperson worth the name can obtain listings using perfectly honest and ethical means. The following techniques will gain you access and win you a good reputation and good will at the same time.

Why Are You There?   You should have a specific reason for ringing a doorbell rather than the very general: "Do you want to sell your house?" This extremely direct approach brings in some listings, but can be greatly improved upon.

The Survey.   A popular approach is to conduct a survey of the area to determine residents' needs:

> "Good morning, Mrs. Smyth. I am Jane Little, an agent with Sunset Realty. Our office is over on Main Street. I would like to give you one of our telephone note pads [hand her the pad]. Our office is in the process of conducting a housing survey in [Sommerset Estates], and I would appreciate very much if you would help me by answering a few questions."

Don't wait for an answer. Assume the response to be yes and continue:

> "Do you own your home, Mrs. Smyth? How long have you lived here? What is the size of your family? What are the ages of your children? Do you consider your home to be well suited to your needs and if not, what changes would you prefer? Do you and Mr. Smyth plan to move within the next five years?"

If the answer is affirmative, ask when and why.

> "Have you or Mr. Smyth given any consideration to selling or buying any property? Do you know of any neighbors or friends who might be interested in selling or buying any real estate?"

> "Have any of your neighbors had a change in their housing needs recently because of marriage, birth, divorce, death, graduation or any other reason?"

If affirmative, get the names and addresses and the person's opinion about whether the neighbors will be selling their home.

> "Since relocation is an important decision, do you think that Mr. and Mrs. Brown would like to receive information about the value of their home? Our office can provide an analysis of value at no cost or obligation to them."

The phrasing of this question is designed to evoke a positive response. You are now in a position to approach the Browns with a referral from a neighbor.

This kind of survey pinpoints the specific needs and motivations of the people you are talking with as well as those of their neighbors and friends. This technique allows you to identify 90 percent of the homes that will be on the market in a given location, even though you only contact 25 percent of the households.

Prospects. Effective though the survey method is, I personally prefer a more specific approach that involves owners with prospective buyers. These prospects become your reason for being there, so you can forget free gifts and other door openers. Always use real prospects:

> "Good morning, Mrs. Smyth. My name is Jane Little. I am an agent with Sunset Realty over on Main Street. Perhaps you can help me. I am looking for a home for a young couple who desire to live in your neighborhood. He is an engineer with Telcon. They particularly like this area because of Grant Park and the Greely Grade School. They have a nine-year-old daughter who currently attends Greely.
>
> Do you know of any of your neighbors who are considering selling or might consider selling their home?
>
> Have any of your neighbors had a change in family size because of marriage, divorce, death, birth or graduation?"

The description of your actual prospects should make the person who answers the door like them and want to help. Be sure the prospects you choose fit the area. In a retirement community, try an approach like this:

"I am looking for a home in your area for a couple from Minnesota who recently retired. He was an accountant with 3M Corporation. The couple likes your area because it is close to Central City where their daughter, son-in-law, and three grandchildren live. Yet, it's far enough away so the children won't feel they are interfering with their lives."

Church Members. Quite by accident I discovered a variation of canvassing for a particular buyer which I feel is the single most effective canvassing technique possible. I was working with a couple who had two children. He worked on Sundays and his wife did not drive. They wanted a home within walking distance of a particular church. At the time there was nothing suitable listed for sale in the area. I stopped at the church and picked up a list of members and their addresses. I contacted several members of the church who lived close by. My approach went something like this:

"Good morning, Mrs. Shepherd. I obtained your name and address from Bethel Lutheran Church. My name is William Pivar and I am a broker with Westwood Realty. I wonder if you can help me. I am trying to find a home for a young couple who need to be within walking distance of Bethel Lutheran Church. He works on Sundays and his wife doesn't drive. They have a son nine years old and a daughter eleven years old who will both be attending the Sunday school.

Do you know anyone in the area who might be interested in selling their home to this young couple, perhaps someone who has had a change in family size or who is planning on leaving the area?"

I was amazed at the positive results I received. After three contacts, calls were being made to all of the members of the Women's Club. I got seven leads and sold one of the two listings I got to the couple I was trying to help.

Because people identify with members of their church, I ask prospects if they would like to be close to any particular house of worship. If they name one, I have a source of willing and eager helpers in the church auxiliary. I consider this an outstanding Power approach.

How to Use a Lead. When your canvassing gives you a lead, contact the party and use the referral as an opening:

> "Good morning, Mrs. Hopkins. My name is Jane Little from Sunset Realty over on Main Street. Mrs. Henderson next door suggested I talk with you.
>
> I have been working with a young couple who desire to live in this neighborhood. He is an engineer with Telcom. They have a young daughter nine years old who goes to Greely School. They like this area because it is close to the school as well as to Grant Park.
>
> Mrs. Henderson suggested that you might be interested in selling your beautiful home. I realize that it's a big decision to make, and I imagine you haven't made up your mind.
>
> Before you make any decisions, you should know the value of your property. I would like to prepare a competitive market analysis for you which will show what you could expect to receive should you decide to sell. We can prepare an analysis without any cost or obligation to you. Would it be all right if I took a look through your home, Mrs. Hopkins?"

This isn't a cold canvass because you have a reason for being there. Mrs. Henderson, a neighbor, suggested you could help Mrs. Hopkins. This is an excellent nonthreatening approach.

Your goal now is an opportunity to perform a competitive market analysis. When you present that you will work for the listing. However, if you find the owner is very receptive at the initial contact, don't be afraid to go for the listing.

"Would You Be Offended?" Tom Hopkins, a great real estate trainer and salesman, is credited with this short and simple, yet unique, Power approach:

> "Would you be offended if I asked to see your house?"
>
> "Would you be offended if I stopped by to see your house?"

Most people are nice people. They would not be offended if you asked to see their home and that is what their answer has to be: an invitation to view the house.

If the same people were asked if you could view their home, they might say, "No we don't want to talk to real estate agents." But the polite "Would you be offended" approach wins them over.

Polaroid Picture. This is a good initial approach for a home that has a For Sale By Owner sign:

> "I hope you don't mind; I took a picture of your home. You can have it [handing it to owner]. Perhaps you would like to use it for a newspaper ad."

The owner is not going to mind that you took a picture of the house. The owner, by getting something, has been placed in a better frame of mind for one of the opening listing presentations.

"If" Offer. This approach is very effective. A saleswoman in an office where I worked used it like this:

> "Mrs. Knowles, I am Agnes Ludwig with Eastside Realty. You wrote an excellent ad on your home. Have you had any advertising experience?"

This compliment can be used in any approach. People generally think they did an excellent job on their ad. Some spend a great deal of time preparing it. A positive response to the compliment gives you a chance to get down to business:

> "Mrs. Knowles, if I had an offer on your house, would you want to see it?"

Of course they would want to see it. We are all curious people, especially when it concerns our property. Again, a positive answer provides an opening:

> "No, I don't have an offer yet, but I very well may be able to get one. I would like to see your property because I feel it

> may meet the needs of one of my prospects, a young couple
> with a 9-year-old daughter. Would it be all right if I stopped
> by at 3 p.m. to view your home? Or would 4 be more con-
> venient?"

This Power approach has led to a natural positive reply.

"I Understand." This Power approach works well when you have
a possible buyer for a For Sale By Owner home. Your telephone or in-person canvass could go like this:

> "Mrs. Lowry, I am James Perkins from Spring Realty. I suppose
> by now you are sick and tired of real estate people trying to list
> your home."

This statement can be dynamite when it follows calls from
several other agents.

> "I understand the reasons why you would want to sell your
> home yourself; however, I am working with a young family with
> two children, a son 8 years old and a daughter 11, and I feel your
> home could meet their needs."

Describe your actual prospects in as favorable a fashion
as possible. A particular buyer makes a much stronger
impression than a vague buyer or buyers in general.

> "If my buyer would pay you full price, would you be willing to
> pay a fee?"

The answer to this request will usually be positive in which
case your next statement would be,

> "Would it be convenient for me to stop by and view your home
> at 5 p.m. today or would 6 p.m. be better for you?"

If the owner is not available at 5 p.m. or 6 p.m., ask,

> "What time would be more convenient for you?"

Should the owner indicate an unwillingness to pay any
commission, even if a full-price offer were received, ask:

"If my buyers would agree to pay my fee, would you allow me to show your home to them?"

This answer *will* result in a positive answer, as the owner will only benefit from such an arrangement. When you are ready to request the right to represent the owner as their agent, you will then emphasize that it is the buyer, not the seller, who actually pays your fee. This is covered in detail in Chapter 5.

For Sale By Owner Kit. A very effective approach, if properly handled, is a For Sale By Owner kit. It takes time and money to prepare, but it will give you entry when all other means fail. It also creates a great deal of goodwill. You can advertise these free kits, which will upset your competition because they don't understand their use, or you can use a phone approach on For Sale By Owner ads:

> "Mr. Hopkins, I am Wilbert Watkins from Country Corner Realty. Have you been able to sell your home yet. Perhaps I can help you sell your home yourself. Our office has put together For Sale By Owner kits which contain a For Sale sign, contracts, loan applications, instructions for open houses and much more. We provide these kits absolutely free as a goodwill gesture. Of course we hope that if you decide later that you want professional help, you will consider us. I would like to deliver one of these free kits to you and show you how to use the forms. Will you and your wife be home at 7 tonight? Or would 8 be more convenient?"

Your kit should include a For Sale By Owner sign, purchase contracts, sample ads, helpful tips on showing, open house signs, loan application forms for local lenders, FHA forms, and several sheets of directions. The material you have assembled should be really helpful. Put WARNING labels on several sheets that talk about subordination clauses, points on loans and other pitfalls.

Give the owner the signs and then sit down together and go over the forms. Go slowly and point out dangers: tying up the property with a buyer who won't qualify for a loan; false credit data; the difference between "seller to pay assessments" and "buyer to assume assessments, the effect of a subordination clause. By the time you finish your presentation, the owners will probably begin to wonder if selling their home themselves is really as simple as they imagined. At that point, ask,

> "What are you asking for your home?"

> "How did you arrive at that figure?"

Usually it is based upon a single sale in the area or what the owners would like to get.

> "It would be presumptuous of me to tell you if the price is high or low, but our firm does competitive market analyses from our computer data. I would like to do one for you, and provide it at no charge."

Now start asking questions and taking measurements. Set an appointment for the next night to present the completed competitive market analysis.

The owners took something free from you which they can see will be helpful, even though you have weakened their resolve to sell the home themselves. You have not tried to talk them into listing with you. You are offering a second freebie which will usually be accepted eagerly. This super Power approach leads naturally to listings.

Rewrite the Ad. Another approach to For Sale By Owner situations works like this:

> "Mrs. Sharp, I am John Davis of Davis Realty. I hope you don't mind, but I read your ad in today's paper and I think I can help you sell your home without using an agent. I have rewritten your ad and I think you will agree it is now more effective."

Now hand the owner a sheet of paper with the owner's ad and the ad you have written. Point out the good points of the owner's ad first, then show the changes you have made, explaining why. Point out that since you have not been in the house, you could not be sure of any additional features to cover. This should get you invited in. If not, go to one of the other entry approaches. The problem with this approach is that you criticize what an owner has done. This could result in a negative reaction no matter how helpful you are. While many salespeople use this approach successfully, I believe there are better ways.

The Owner Open House. An owner's open house sign gives you a natural entry. I recommend stopping by at about 4:30 on a Sunday afternoon. By then the owners probably have had a disappointing day waiting for buyers. Rather than trying for the opportunity to conduct a competitive market analysis, see if the owners are ready to talk about why they need an agent. You want to catch the owners while they are still in a receptive mood.

When the Owner Invites You. If you are invited to talk about a sale, go for the listing on your first contact. Assume you will get the listing. Bring a listing form on your clipboard; as you get information, put it on the form. If owners get upset that you are filling out a listing, tell them it's simply a convenient way to set down property information. Reserve this approach for contacts based on a previous relationship with you or your firm. If the contact is from canvassing, build a level of trust and demonstrate your ability before you try for a listing.

IN THE HOUSE

When you get into a home look around for something to compliment the owner on. If an item of furniture or a decorative piece looks as if it doesn't belong, it probably has a special meaning or significance to an owner. If there is a trophy displayed, the owner wants it to be noticed and praised.

People like people who are interested in things they like. If you can't find anything unusual, consider the exterior of the house. If the landscaping looks well-cared for, compliment the owner on it. If new plantings are going in, ask about them—be interested. If nothing else, comment on a picture of the children or on the dress or grooming of the owner(s).

Get excited about the property. The owners will be pleased that you like their property. I believe one of the reasons women are likely to be more successful in listing and selling homes is their ability to show their interest. Men act out the emotionless male stereotype and fail to show enthusiasm, thus losing the opportunity to win the goodwill of owners.

As you go through the house ask questions, be interested in the details the owner provides, take notes. Walk around the outside of the house; be extremely curious. On a large lot, walk the boundaries. To show your interest you can even pick up soil around plants and examine it.

Offering the Competitive Market Analysis. Whether or not you know the price the owners have set, ask them. Then ask how they arrived at that price. You should not be argumentative, just interested.

The owners probably based their price on very unscientific notions: one actual or supposed sale in the neighborhood, what the owners feel they have invested in the home, or an arbitrary figure the owners would love to get but won't. Whatever the basis, now is the time to try for a competitive market analysis:

> "It would be presumptuous of me or any real estate professional to tell you that the price is either too high or too low without a competitive market analysis. In a competitive market analysis we analyze comparable homes that sold and that didn't sell. We show their list prices, actual sale prices, terms, and even how long it took to procure a buyer. With this analysis we are able to predict the actual price range in which your home should sell, and the most effective sale terms. Our office prepares such an analysis at no cost or obligation. Before I show your home, I would like to prepare a competitive market analysis for you."

Assume that the answer is yes and start asking questions and taking notes. Measure rooms, having an owner hold one end of the tape measure. Getting the owner involved can help lessen whatever resistance the owner still has. The owner wants to feel that you have considered all of his or her labor and improvements, so let him or her tell all while you write it down. You may be able to give a good estimate of the house's value, but the owner wants to feel you've appreciated all the special features and factored them into the value of the property.

When you have completed your questions and measurements, ask the owners,

> "Mr. and Mrs. Clyde, I can come back tomorrow evening at 8 to show you both the results of the analysis. Is that convenient with you or would you prefer 9 p.m.?"

If the owners have small children, be certain to schedule your meeting after they have gone to bed. You want to make your presentation with as few interruptions as possible.

Try to put a hold on things with this suggestion:

> "I suggest you remove your For Sale sign [or 'delay showing your home']. You wouldn't want to sell your home for less than our analysis could reveal to be the proper price?"

The above statement could help keep your competitors away. You now have a definite appointment to make a presentation on your competitive market analysis. This Power approach opens the way to selling the owners on listing and on you as their agent.

The next chapter explains how to prepare the competitive market analysis and how to produce other aids to convince owners that it is in their best interest to have you represent them in the sale of their home.

4

Power Presentation Aids

You've effectively applied the techniques in Chapter 3 to get an appointment with the owners. Your foot is in the door: you have your chance to sell the owners on why they need you to help them sell their property. The presentation that makes this case must accomplish two things: it must sell the owners on using a broker, and then convince them that you are the best agent for their purposes.

The first part of the process is the most difficult because you must overcome the common but false belief that selling a home without a broker will save the owners money. You must also convince the owners that obtaining professional help is in their best interest, that selling a house involves much more than simply placing a sign on the front lawn and running a few ads.

When you've accomplished this, the hardest part is over, but don't assume that the owners will automatically choose you to represent them. Your firm's fine reputation in the area gives you a big lead over the competition, but the owners will make their decision on the basis of their reaction to what you say and do. To them, you are the firm. Always assume you are in a competitive situation until the agreement is signed.

This chapter provides examples of presentation aids you can prepare to give you a clear competitive advantage. The following chapter shows you how to use the aids to make a winning presentation.

THE COMPETITIVE MARKET ANALYSIS

Chances are that your promise of a competitive market analysis was the reason the owners gave you an opportunity to make your presentation. Don't disappoint them by just assembling a group of current, sold, and expired listings of comparable properties. Very few salespeople could make an effective presentation with so little preparation, and even they'd be hurting their chances of getting the listing.

The Analysis Form. A far better presentation tool is a completed form like the one shown on pages 76 and 77. This shows comparable properties presently for sale, as well as comparable properties that sold and failed to sell during their listing periods.

The completed competitive market analysis form contains much important data but does not really reflect the effort that went into its preparation. It makes your work for the owner look too simple and easy.

The Look of Importance. Some years ago I discovered the importance of making a report *appear* as important and complex as the data shows that it *is*. I did quite a bit of real estate consulting, primarily in sales training. In many cases I could analyze a program and make recommendations for program modifications after a few hours of study. I found that this did not always make my clients happy. I was an outsider seeing at a glance that programs they took years to develop were all wrong. They'd pay me a few hundred dollars plus expenses, then promptly forget the advice they'd just bought.

A friend who did engineering consulting work told *me* in just a few minutes what *I* was doing wrong. My recommendations, he said, did not look valuable enough: my few typed pages didn't reflect the experience that went into their preparation.

My friend, on the other hand, would spend a week or more with his clients, studying procedures, inspecting equipment and methods, and asking hundreds of questions at every level. About a month after he left, he'd present a dozen bound copies of a formal report to the firm's executives. The report would carefully analyze alternative solutions, make definite recommendations, and present supporting data dressed up in color graphs, photographs and other lavish graphics. Clients who paid his four-figure bills followed his advice. What he gave *looked* as valuable as it *was*.

I tried his approach, taking more time, dressing up my reports, making a formal presentation, and raising my fees. The requests for my services increased and firms were much happier with the work I did for them.

This experience can increase your listing power just as effectively as it boosted my consulting success, as the records of hundreds of my former students proves. They have found that owners feel an obligation to an agent who spends so much care and effort on their behalf.

The example, shown on pages 78 through 87, shows what can be done with some of the same information we used in the short form. In a real presentation, the report would be inserted in a cover from a printer or stationer, or even in a spiral-bound booklet custom-made by your printer at relatively little cost.

Establishing Value.   Appraisal is not an exact science that can predict definite sales prices. We can, however, predict a reasonable range of values. This limitation actually turns out to be an advantage: a price range prepares owners for an offer anywhere in that range, so an offer in the lower area still comes through as reasonable. An offer $2,000 below the range would really be only $2,000 less than your appraisal.

COMPETITIVE MARKET ANALYSIS

PROPERTY BEING EVALUATED: 9736 W. Elm St., 3 BR, 2 BA., Den, Oversize 2-car garage
Approx. 1820 sq. ft., 9 yrs. old

COMPARABLES	AGE	SQUARE FEET	BEDROOMS	BATHS	DEN/FAMILY ROOM	ASSUMABLE LOANS	TERMS	LIST PRICE	DAYS AVAILABLE	ACTUAL SALE PRICE & TERMS
FOR SALE										
4813 W. Elm includes sauna	4	1900	4	2	—	—	owner will finance 10% down	$108,000	37	
2111 32nd Street large patio, exc. landscaping	9	1820	3	2	D	$46,000	submit	$118,000	87	
5817 Beech needs decorating	4	2000	3	2½	D	$52,000	owner will carry 7 yrs. lge. dwn. pmt.	$120,000	114	
1218 Diamond Ct. on Cul de Sac, 3-car garage	New	1950	3	2	D	—	cash to seller	$120,000	156	
SOLD-(WITHIN LAST 6 MOS. UNLESS INDICATED)										
4912 Poplar St.	5	1900	3	2	D	$52,000	submit	$110,000	37	owner took $30,000 2nd-12% $105,500

Property										
4642 Elm similar to 9736 Elm, exc.cond.	9	1900	3	2	D	$81,000	cash to loan	$100,000	16	$19,000 cash $100,000
4113 Pine	3	1950	4	2½	–	$29,000	submit owner will carry	$108,000	46	$10,000 down L.C.–11% $99,500
3973 Kings Hwy.		2000	3	2	D	–	cash to seller	$112,000	64	cash to seller $102,000
EXPIRED-UNSOLD (WITHIN LAST 6 MOS.)										
3822 Lincoln separate Dining Room	7	1940	3	2	–	–	submit	$122,000	120	
2711 Highland	6	1910	3	2½	D	–	submit	$114,000	90	
4613 Oak slab for camper	2	2000	3	2	FR	$63,000	cash to loan	$115,000	120	
3763 Hickory spa in patio area	5	1920	3	2½	–	–	submit all offers	$119,500	120	

AGENT'S EVALUATION – From the data presented, it is the professional opinion of the undersigned that the property at 9736 W. Elm will sell within a range from $98,500 to $106,000.

4-6-83
date

Thomas Fliggins

Thomas Fliggins
Associate Broker
Clyde Realty

COMPETITIVE MARKET ANALYSIS

Prepared for

Thomas and Irene Jones

Property location:

9736 W. Elm Street

Boonville, CA.

Date of report 9—24—82

Prepared by: Clyde Realty
                   7381 Elk Road
                   Boonville, CA. 90831

REPORT BACKGROUND

In preparing this report the Joneses' home was compared with 12 other homes which, in the opinion of our office, are comparable in value to the home at 9736 W. Elm Street.

In determining these comparables, the extra features of the Joneses' home was added to the home, and its excellent overall condition and fine location were fully considered.

While individual features of these homes vary, they are all considered in the same general range as to buyer desirability.

We have selected the comparables in three categories:

1. Homes presently available.

2. Homes that have been sold in the last 6 months.

3. Homes where the listings expired unsold within the last 6 months.

9736 W. Elm Street
Boonville, California

General Description of Property

3 bedroom, 2 bath and den home.
Stucco construction. Oversized 2-car attached garage.
Approximately 1,820 square feet.
Home is 9 years old.

Area

Very desirable northside subdivision. The home is
only 2 blocks from Hi Mount Grade School and 6
blocks from the Midvale Middle School. The new
Plaza Center is planned less than one mile away.

Special Features

The living room has a massive Tennessee Stone
fireplace. Exceptionally well maintained home
and grounds with six fruit trees and towering
date palms. Automatic garage door openers,
automatic sprinkler system. Built-in cabinets
and workshop in garage.

(This page should indicate you appreciate the
owner's home.)

Comparable Homes Presently on the Market

4813 W. Elm Street

This 1,900 square foot home is 4 years old. While it has 4 bedrooms, there is no den. It has 2 baths and a double garage. Included in the sale is a 60 sq. ft. redwood sauna in the back yard. The exterior needs painting and the landscaping is average. The owner will finance with 10% down.

List price: $108,000
Days on Market: 37

2111 - 32nd Street

This 9 year old home was built by Conboy Builders, the same builders who built the Joneses' home. It has the same general floor plan and has been kept up well. The house has a large concrete patio and exceptional landscaping. The owners have indicated they will help finance.

List price: $118,000
Days on Market: 87

5817 Beech Street

This 3 bedroom and den, 2½ bath home has approx.
2,000 sq. ft. and a double garage. The home needs
complete interior redecorating including new
carpeting. The home is 4 years old. Owner will
carry loan at 9% for 7 years with substantial
down payment.

List price: $120,000
Days on Market: 114

1218 Diamond Court

This new 3 bedroom and den, 2 bath home has 1,950
sq. ft. and has a three-car garage. The home is
located on the end of a quiet cul-de-sac. The
house has not been landscaped. No seller financing
is available.

List price: $120,000
Days on Market: 156

Comparable Sales—Last 6 Months

4912 Poplar Street

This 3 bedroom and den, 2 bath home has 1,900 sq. ft.
It is 5 years old. The buyer assumed the seller's
$52,000, 8% 1st mortgage and the seller carried back
a $30,000, 2nd mortgage at 12% interest.

List price: $110,000
Actual sale price: $103,500
Days on Market: 37

4642 Elm Street

While a different floor plan, this 3 bedroom 2 bath
home with oversize double garage was built at the
same time as the home at 4737 Elm by the same
builder. It has approx. 1,900 sq. ft. and was
in excellent overall condition. Buyer paid $19,000
down and assumed seller's $81,000 loan at 11%
interest.

List price: $110,000
Actual sale price: $100,000
Days on Market: 16

4113 Pine Street

This 4 bedroom, 2 bath home with 2½ car garage is 3 years old and has 1,950 sq. ft. It was in very fine condition. The owner sold it on land contract at 11½% interest with $10,000 down.

List price: $108,000
Actual sale price: $ 99,500
Days on Market: 46

3973 Kings Highway

This 3 bedroom and den, 2 bath home has a 2-car garage and is located on an oversize corner lot. The house has approx. 2,000 sq. ft. It was sold-all cash.

List price: $112,000
Actual sale price: $102,000
Days on Market: 64

Comparable Homes Where Listings Expired Unsold

3822 Lincoln

This 3 bedroom 2 bath, double garage home has 1,940 sq. ft. A separate dining room (not area) which could be converted into a den. It is in very good condition. Owner indicated "submit as to terms."

List price: $122,000
Days on Market: 120
UNSOLD

2711 Highland

This 1,910 sq. foot home has 3 bedrooms and den, 2½ baths plus a double garage. Owner was willing to finance.

List price: $114,000
Days on Market: 90
UNSOLD

4613 Oak Street

This 2 year old, 3 bedroom 2 bath home has large
rooms and a separate family room. It has a 2-car
garage plus a side slab for a camper. It has
approx. 2,000 sq. ft. Owner wanted cash to
$63,000 loan.

List price: $115,000
Days on Market: 120
UNSOLD

3763 Hickory Street

This 3 bedroom, 2½ bath, double garage home has
1,920 sq. ft. It has desert landscaping and a
spa in the patio area. Owner stated "submit
all offers."

List price: $119,500
Days on Market: 120
UNSOLD

Based on the competitive market analysis, it is the opinion of the undersigned that the sale price of the home at 9736 W. Elm Street will be in the range between $98,500 and $106,000.

All information contained herein was prepared for Thomas and Irene Jones. The material is considered confidential and was prepared solely to evaluate the home at 9736 W. Elm Street.

Data provided was obtained from the Boonville Board of Realtors.

Opinions presented are those of Clyde Realty.

Prepared by _____
                    Thomas Fliggins
                    Associate Broker

Approved _____
                    Walter Clyde
                    Broker

Your competitive market survey will reveal that whatever the list prices of comparables, the selling prices end up about the same. A high list price will not bring a sale above the property's fair market value.

The average list prices of unsold homes will undoubtedly be significantly higher than the ones for homes that were sold. The analysis will clearly reveal that setting an unrealistically high price does not help the owners: overpriced listings are less likely to sell at any price than listings priced competitively from the start.

Your analysis will reveal that owners do best by pricing the home as close to actual sale prices as possible, rather than to the list prices of comparables. Properties with realistic list prices attract more buyers, sell faster, and close at figures just as high as those of overpriced competitors.

If the actual sale price of one of your comparables seems out of line, check it out with the selling broker. There may be unusual seller or buyer motivation, special problems or benefits, or terms or special features not indicated in the information you have.

If FHA or lender appraisal information is available, include it in your competitive market analysis. For example, "FHA Appraisal 10/26/82: $93,500."

Formats. Some multiple-listing services provide computer print-out data which can be attached to or included as part of your competitive market analysis if it is readable enough. Actual listings are best left out because their formats tend to confuse owners. I recommend putting the important data in readable form, as in the sample analysis. If you specialize in a price range or area, you will use many of the same comparables for several analyses and find your preparation time greatly reduced.

Some salespeople prefer showing just the bare data because it allows easier preparation and comparison. Such a bare descriptive format follows:

4613 Oak Street	$115,000
Days on market	120

3 bedrooms

2 baths

2 years old

2-car garage plus parking pad

approximately 2,000 square feet

Financing — cash to existing $63,000 loan

In describing each property, I prefer the narrative approach that I described. By making each property seem more desirable, it helps prepare the owner for a realistic list price and terms.

One of my former students shows the relationship between list price and the likelihood of a sale by a graph like this:

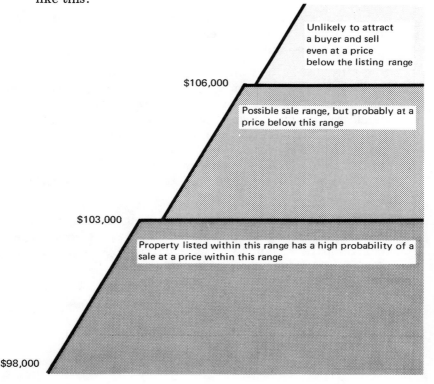

Unlikely to attract a buyer and sell even at a price below the listing range

$106,000

Possible sale range, but probably at a price below this range

$103,000

Property listed within this range has a high probability of a sale at a price within this range

$98,000

THE LISTING PRESENTATION BOOK

Many offices provide their salespeople with listing presentation books designed to sell their firm and the advantages of employing an agent. A presentation book provides a visual display as you make your presentation, and keeps you from leaving out any of the important special advantages of using real estate brokers, and your firm in particular. Such a book enables you to make a smooth, effective presentation every time.

Some offices use elaborate video presentations rather than presentation books. Despite the professionalism of these presentations, I believe a presentation book is far more effective. The television set doesn't sell you or your personality. It doesn't emphasize an owner's particular interests. It can't respond to the owner's reactions. Owners don't give listings to television sets; they give them to people.

If you use a book prepared by your firm, I recommend adding a page about yourself. Keep in mind that to most owners you are your firm.

Most listing presentation books are divided into two sections, one on the firm and the other on reasons to list, in that order. I believe that this is the wrong approach. You should sell owners on why they need an agent before you sell yourself as that agent. The first few minutes of your presentation are the most important. Use them to provide Power reasons to use an agent. Otherwise the owners will be thinking of ways to get rid of you before you've even shown them why using an agent will benefit them.

Presentation books generally appear in a ringed binder with each sheet protected in plastic. The sample book, beginning on page 91, shows an effective arrangement that emphasizes all the important selling points.

WHY DO

MOST PEOPLE BUY

REAL ESTATE

THROUGH LICENSED

PROFESSIONALS?

What does this sign attract?

1.   **Unqualified lookers**

2.   **Bargain hunters**

3.   **Many real estate agents**

4.

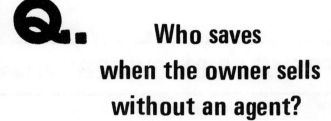

Q. Who saves
when the owner sells
without an agent?

A. The buyer.

"FOR SALE BY OWNER" means

1. **Time wasted**

2. **Problems of negotiation**

3. **Problems of finances**

4. **Likelihood of legal problems**

5. **Likelihood of financial loss**

6. **Likelihood of failure**

Most owners who

try to sell their own

property

end up engaging a

professional agent

because:

AGENTS SELL

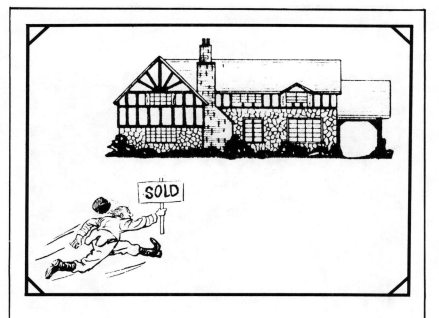

I CAN HELP YOU!

I have helped hundreds of homeowners sell their homes
14 years of successful real estate experience in our community

Thomas Green, CRS
Certified Residential Specialist
Associate Broker
Clyde Realty

OUR TEAM

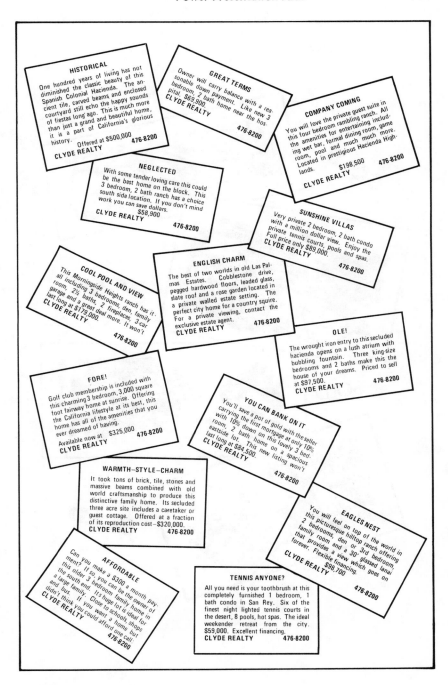

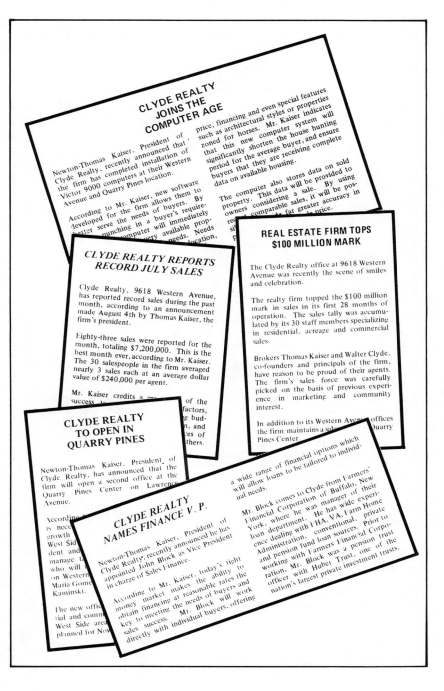

CLYDE REALTY JOINS THE COMPUTER AGE

Newton-Thomas Kaiser, President of Clyde Realty, recently announced that the firm has completed installation of Victor 9000 computers at their Western Avenue and Quarry Pines location.

According to Mr. Kaiser, new software developed for the firm allows them to better serve the needs of buyers. By punching in a buyer's requirements, the computer will immediately display every available property. Needs such as location,

price, financing and even special features such as architectural styles or properties zoned for horses. Mr. Kaiser indicates that this new computer system will significantly shorten the house hunting period for the average buyer, and ensure buyers that they are receiving complete data on available housing.

The computer also stores data on sold property. This data will be provided to owners considering a sale. By using recent comparable sales, it will be possible to set a more accurate price.

REAL ESTATE FIRM TOPS $100 MILLION MARK

The Clyde Realty office at 9618 Western Avenue was recently the scene of smiles and celebration.

The realty firm topped the $100 million mark in sales in its first 28 months of operation. The sales tally was accumulated by its 30 staff members specializing in residential, acreage and commercial sales.

Brokers Thomas Kaiser and Walter Clyde, co-founders and principals of the firm, have reason to be proud of their agents. The firm's sales force was carefully picked on the basis of previous experience in marketing and community interest.

In addition to its Western Avenue offices the firm maintains a sales office in Quarry Pines Center.

CLYDE REALTY REPORTS RECORD JULY SALES

Clyde Realty, 9618 Western Avenue, has reported record sales during the past month, according to an announcement made August 4th by Thomas Kaiser, the firm's president.

Eighty-three sales were reported for the month, totaling $7,200,000. This is the best month ever, according to Mr. Kaiser. The 30 salespeople in the firm averaged nearly 3 sales each at an average dollar value of $240,000 per agent.

Mr. Kaiser credits a number of the success to a number of factors, including budget, location, and prices of others.

CLYDE REALTY TO OPEN IN QUARRY PINES

Newton-Thomas Kaiser, President of Clyde Realty, has announced that the firm will open a second office at the Quarry Pines Center on Lawrence Avenue.

According to Kaiser, the new office is necessary to accommodate the growth of the West Side residential development and to manage the properties who will be handled on Western Avenue by Maria Gomez and Kaminski.

The new office residential and commercial West Side area is planned for November.

CLYDE REALTY NAMES FINANCE V. P.

Newton-Thomas Kaiser, President of Clyde Realty, recently announced he has appointed John Block as Vice President in charge of Sales Finance.

According to Mr. Kaiser, today's tight money market makes the ability to obtain financing at reasonable rates the key to meeting the needs of buyers and sales success. Mr. Block will work directly with individual buyers, offering a wide range of financial options which will allow loans to be tailored to individual needs.

Mr. Block comes to Clyde from Farmers' Financial Corporation of Buffalo, New York, where he was manager of their loan department. He has wide experience dealing with FHA, VA, Farm Home Administration, conventional, private and pension fund loan sources. Prior to working with Farmers' Financial Corporation, Mr. Block was a pension trust officer with Huber Trust, one of the nation's largest private investment trusts.

JEROME MACK

Builder of Better Homes
9000 Sierra Way
Palmview, CA 97608
(619) 820-4737

Thomas Kaiser
Clyde Realty
9618 Western Avenue
Newton, CA 97603

Dear Mr. Kaiser,

In my business I am used to dealing with people who promise the moon but seem to be stricken with a terminal loss of memory as soon as an agreement is signed.

I am very happy to say that this was not the case in dealing with your saleswoman, Joan Webb. She was both professional and realistic. Your office performed as she indicated it would. My dealings with your office has reaffirmed my faith in real estate brokers.

I will be starting two new "spec" homes next month. As soon as my costs are firmed up, I will contact Joan. I hope that this is the start of a long and mutually rewarding association with your firm.

Yours truly,

Jerry Mack

Jerry Mack

JM:cem

Joan Webb
Clyde Realty

Dear Joan,
We were so busy at the closing that
I did not have the opportunity to
properly thank you for your help
in selling Mother's home.

I had no idea as to the depth
of knowledge required in so many
areas in order to properly sell a
home. As a neophyte, I really appreciated the time you spent
with me explaining the various
alternatives available. The all-
inclusive mortgage provides
Mother with an annuity which
more than doubles her social
security. It was just what she wanted.

Again, many thanks,
Elizabeth Huber
P.S. Mother is sending you a rum cake. Enjoy it.

Colonel Alexander Patterson, USA

APO 190

New York, NY   07014

Joan Webb
Clyde Realty
9618 Western Avenue
Newton, CA   97603

Dear Ms. Webb,

It is with great pleasure that I write this letter to
congratulate you and your firm, not only on the
professional manner that you showed in the sale of my
home, but also for the assistance you provided my wife.

As a service wife, Emily has gone through previous
home sales in my absence. However, in no previous
instance did she encounter salespeople and brokers who
really placed our interests above all others. Because
Emily desired to join me as soon as possible, she was
willing to accept the first offer you presented. We
are now very happy that you advised her against
acceptance. Your advice made a substantial difference
in our present financial picture. Rather than just
getting our money out of the house, you were able to
put together an exceptional transaction.

I want you to know that I really appreciate what you
did for us. If you ever need a reference, don't
hesitate to call on us.

Alexander Patterson
Col. Alexander Patterson, USA

Include a copy of the cover sheet of your errors and omissions policy if it looks impressive, under a heading like this:

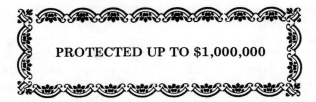

PROTECTED UP TO $1,000,000

Selling Your Firm. Your presentation book should sell specific advantages of your firm. Each major point is on a separate sheet in large type. Use photographs where appropriate.

Here are some points to emphasize:

Size. If your firm is small, tell how you specialize in selling a few properties, rather than hundreds. If your firm is large, point out the size as an asset.

Affiliation. If your firm is a member of a franchise, point it out. If your firm is a member of a multiple-listing service and/or a referral service, point this out. If your firm is completely independent, point it out as an asset.

Satisfied customers. As you saw in the presentation book, testimonial letters from former buyers and sellers are very effective, especially if they are from people known and respected in the community. Try to have letters from a variety of people so you can call attention to the one that especially relates to your prospect.

Sales. If your firm has had many sales, point this out. A very positive approach is to compare your record to an MLS service average: "We offer a 17% greater likelihood of a successful sale than the average for the Westside Board of Realtors." The chances are that you will beat the board average—it includes many unrealistic listings.

Percentage of your personal sales of your own listings. "I work on my listings. Sixty-eight percent of my own sales are my own listings."

Percent of your own listings which have sold. "Over the last two years, 72 percent of my listings have sold within 90 days." This is important to emphasize when your own rate is much higher than your office rate. It can be dangerous to point out the actual percentage of your sold listings. You may be proud of your 60 percent sales rate, but an owner could see a 40 percent failure rate.

Other points:

• Your office's home purchase plan, under which you will buy homes.

• Your office's offer of a Home Protection Warranty, which attracts buyers.

• If your office has been in business a long time, put a caption on an early photograph of your office: "Meeting the needs of Oakridge since 1942."

• You have developed excellent relations with lenders so you have sources of conventional and private loans.

• The ratio of sale price to listing price for either yourself or your office is high.

• If you specialize in an area, show a map with a caption, "Specializing in Oakridge."

• Your average sale takes less time than the average time for your multiple-listing service: "Our average sale is 41 days after listing compared to an area average of 63 days."

• "We get you more money. Our sales in December yielded owners an average of 93½ percent of the list price, compared with 83 percent for our multiple-listing service."

Every office has positive points. Your multiple-listing service data will suggest many areas where you can show your superior performance. How to call attention to specific advantages of your firm is discussed in greater depth in the next chapter.

5
Power Presentation Strategies

Armed with your presentation book, you begin the task of showing an owner why he or she should list, and why you are the agent who can serve the owner's purpose best. You'll usually find more resistance to the idea of giving a listing at all than to giving one to you in particular. If you can sell the owners on using an agent, you will most likely be able to sell yourself as that agent. This chapter takes you through the presentation process, explaining the Power techniques that will enable you to turn owners into listers who name you as their representative.

You've probably gotten past the door by promising a competitive market analysis, so this is what the owners are waiting to hear about. Presenting it with the aid of your prepared copy is quite simple. You can go through the pages with the owners, reading it aloud and explaining, where appropriate, why you selected the homes you did, and their special features.

Your presentation of the analysis should put your prospects in a receptive mood, since you have obviously spent a great deal of time and effort on their behalf. They will almost certainly feel obligated to listen to your discussion [don't use the term *presentation*—it emphasizes the idea that you are trying to sell something].

The best use of the mood you have created is to go into the *Why List* presentation immediately after the analysis, since most owners want to avoid paying a commission. There are times, however, that call for delaying this portion of the presentation. When owners are not opposed to the idea of giving a listing, you can go right to the *Why Us* presentation explained beginning on page 120. Use the same strategy with an owner upset over the price you've recommended in the analysis. He or she will not be listening to what you say now, so sell him or her on yourself first, then on letting you list the property.

SETTING THE MOOD

Coordinate your listing presentation with your presentation book. This way you appeal to the senses of sight as well as sound. The use of the book will serve as a prompter for a smooth presentation. Turning to a new page for each of the reasons can be very effective. The presentation book in Chapter 4 is a model only. Your book's reasons to list, and their order, should follow the form you feel most comfortable with.

Most salespeople have the owners sit side by side and turn the pages of the presentation book from the other side of the kitchen table. I recommend you sit in the middle, with both of the owners close to you. Psychologically this closeness can go a long way toward breaking down barriers.

APPROACHING THE RELUCTANT LISTENER

Should an owner indicate that he or she doesn't have time to talk now or doesn't want to discuss listing the home, I recommend the ten-minute approach:

> "I know you are busy but could you spare me just ten minutes of your time?"

Take off your watch and place it on the kitchen table as you are asking. This approach will normally get you your ten minutes. If you have an alarm watch, setting it for ten minutes can be effective. By the time the alarm goes off, you should have been able to get the owners interested. Now say,

> "I have used up my ten minutes and if you wish I will leave, but would it be all right if I continue?"

This statement shows the owners you are not threatening. Your honest and logical approach during your first ten minutes should have been well received. You should have weakened the owners' resolve against employing an agent. If you are getting the owners' interest at all, you will be asked to continue.

Often owners—out of simple politeness rather than interest—will give you additional time because most people are nice people. Some salespeople use the ten-minute approach in every presentation. After they have gone over the competitive market analysis, they ask,

> "Would it be all right if I took just ten minutes of your time to cover some aspects of selling your home which you may not have considered?"

The owners will invariably respond positively: after all, you have just completed some valuable research for them. They are, in fact, now inviting you to make your presentation.

WHY LIST?

When your prospects are in a mood to listen receptively, you have won the chance to achieve the most difficult goal of the listing process: convincing them that they will be better off selling their house through an agent than on their own. To do this, you must shatter the myth that they can save money by bypassing the broker. Your tools for the task are the reasons presented in this section. Read them carefully over and over, until they become second nature to you and you can smoothly present them in ways that suit any situation. You'll probably find it most effective to save at least one good reason for later, in case the owner needs a final clincher to make a decision. When you become intimately familiar with these reasons to list, you will also develop an instinct for which ones to use with particular homeowners, and where in your selling process each one will be most effective.

How Did You Buy? You want the owners to admit that they purchased this property, or another property, through a real estate agent:

> "Mr. and Mrs. Schneider, when you purchased this home did you deal through a real estate broker?"

Most people do. Keep in mind that developer sales are usually broker sales. If the answer is yes, continue:

> "Wasn't the reason you went to a real estate broker that you were a serious buyer and wanted to see what was available on the market? It was much easier to go through brokers who offered a choice. They had inventories of many homes to choose from."

This is obviously true. The owners will recognize it as a reason they contacted an agent.

> "Well, serious buyers are no different today than you were when you purchased your home. Serious buyers contact real estate professionals."

This Power approach makes owners think. It should be used regularly.

Who Saves the Fee? Here is a strong statement designed to further weaken the idea that For Sale By Owner attempts save money for the seller:

> "If you are successful in selling your home yourself, you won't save any agents' fees. Buyers who contact owners directly know that you won't be paying any fees, so no matter what price you ask or what they consider to be a fair price, they will want to cut that amount by the fee you saved. They won't even agree to split it with you.
>
> These buyers feel that it is the buyer, not the seller, who pays the fees and that they should benefit when an agent is not involved. They are really right. The price they pay includes brokers' fees. Fees are paid out of their money. If an agent is not involved, the buyer feels that fees are not justified.
>
> The net received by owners who sell direct without agents is likely to be less than the net received had agents been employed. Isn't what you actually net from the sale more important to you than whether or not an agent received a fee?"

This is an area where you should come on with power. You are not going to help owners by allowing them to avoid paying brokerage fees. They will not save money, and may actually lose it. In 1974 I made a study of the sale prices of 1,000 homes, 500 of which were sold By Owner and 500 of which were sold through agents. Cooperating escrow offices matched each home sold by an agent with one sold By Owner in the same area.

My 500 broker-involved sales had an average price after brokerage fees of $42,730. The 500 non-broker sales showed an average sale price of $40,947, or almost $2,000 less. While my study did not evaluate amenities, the large number of homes involved assures an accurate picture of actual results. My study proved to me that owners do not save by selling By Owner. More often they actually lose when they "save the commission."

The Classified Ads. You can use classified ads for a simple Power approach. Bring several pages of your local classified ads with all broker ads outlined in one color, and For Sale By Owner ads outlined in a contrasting color. If the owner has advertised with a For Sale By Owner ad, this page should be used with the owner's ad marked. Show the pages to the owner and ask,

> "Why do you suppose most of the ads are by agents?"
>
> "Most people have found that if they want to buy or sell, working through an agent is to their best advantage. Most of these ads currently circled in green will eventually be represented by agents. Do you know why? They will choose agents because they will be unsuccessful in selling their homes."

Why Buyers Like Agents. The likelihood that serious buyers will ignore For Sale By Owner publicity provides a strong supporting reason for using an agent:

> "Legitimate buyers prefer to deal through agents because they know agents can either answer their questions or know where to find the answer.
>
> They know that with a broker involved, a property can be purchased at its listed price. These buyers realize that some owners are unpredictable and might try to raise the price when a buyer shows an interest. These buyers also know that many homes advertised as being For Sale By Owner are not really for sale. Many owners are not serious sellers. They are just testing the market. Just as an unqualified buyer can waste your time, an owner who is not motivated to sell can waste the time of a serious buyer."

Warning: Sharp Operators Ahead. For Sale By Owner ads and signs can attract sharpies who know how to overwhelm the typical homeowner. This approach is especially powerful with owners who have already talked to such operators:

> "While you will find some legitimate buyers attracted to For Sale By Owner ads and signs, more likely you will attract sharp operators who will try to take your property away for less than it is worth. They might offer trades of near-worthless property, jewels, or promissory notes, or attempt any one of several dozen schemes which could leave you with nothing. For example, a current scheme is to get you to agree to carry back part of the purchase price. There is nothing wrong with that, but they insert

one word: *subordinate.* This means your lien will be last. These operators then refinance the loan on your house, get cash, and walk away leaving you with your house and a huge debt which you must pay or lose everything. Unfortunately, there are people who will try to con you out of your property while posing as legitimate buyers. Without professional help you can be a sheep waiting to be shorn. You get a great deal more from a real estate fee than just a legitimate buyer. You also get protection against the sharp operator.

Buyers realize that they must expect to pay a fair price when an agent is involved. They are not going to steal anything. We are experts at getting the most for property. We represent you. We won't let you get pushed into any sale that is not in your best interest.''

It would be unethical to scare a person unnecessarily by warning of nonexistent threats. However, the dangers I have mentioned are very real. I would rather be accused of using scare tactics to obtain a listing than fail to obtain the listing and have owners cheated out of their home equities by sharp operators.

Helping the Owner. Asking helpful questions can be a subtle way to remind owners of the complications they'll have to handle if they sell on their own:

"How much of a deposit do you intend to take with an offer?"

"What form are you going to use to take an offer?"

Don't criticize the owners for being ill prepared. Help them. Show them what they need. You want the owners to realize that selling a home isn't something anyone can do.

Lawsuits. Owners want a simple, uncomplicated sale. This fact makes the following very effective:

"Owners who sell property themselves frequently fail to write complete agreements. They leave out part of the terms or depend on verbal statements. They tend to be trusting. Consequently, owners selling their own property are far more likely to get involved in a lawsuit than if they had an agent. Because dishonest buyers know most owners are unfamiliar with contracts, they make offers that don't really say what they appear to. In fact, the owners often find that they have a far different agreement than they thought. As agents, our job is to protect your interests.

Lookers and No-Shows. Most owners who put their addresses or phone numbers in ads and signs feel at least some discomfort at exposing themselves to unknown prospective buyers. Here is an approach that emphasizes that they have reason to be uneasy:

> "Prospects tend to stop at homes that are priced beyond their budgets. They are like eternal optimists hoping they will find the champagne house to fit their beer budgets. When they find that the price is more than they can afford, they will hesitate to admit it. They will go through your home out of either politeness or curiosity and waste a lot of your time while you falsely believe you have a hot prospect.
>
> Your newspaper ads attract an opposite group of people. We have found that most people buy homes which cost considerably more than the homes they first called on from the ads. Again, they are hoping to find a bargain, a home worth considerably more than your price would indicate. For Sale By Owner signs and ads attract buyers, but seldom qualified buyers, for the home advertised.
>
> When you get a call about your ad, you have to give the caller an address. Have you had anyone call and not show up? [If the owners have had such an experience, this is a super argument.] This is common in owner sales. What happens is that they cruise by. If the exterior doesn't excite them, they don't stop. Buyers are strange animals. While they want to buy, they are often afraid to make a decision. Often they look for excuses not to come to your door. They seldom even show the courtesy of cancelling their appointment."

We Do More Than Advertise. This approach contrasts the problems described in the previous approach with the expert techniques used by the professional:

> "When we get a call about an ad, we meet with the buyers and qualify them as to needs and financial ability. We won't waste

time showing a home when the prospect cannot afford it or the property fails to meet the prospect's needs. More often than not a person who calls about an ad will be switched to another property that better suits his or her needs.

We take our prospects to the homes. We keep them captive; they don't have the option of a drive-by. They see the homes we intend to show.

You benefit not only from our ads, but from the ads placed by every other broker in our multiple listing service. These ads all bring in buyers. We know that prospects seldom buy the home they first inquired about. Usually after the buyers' needs become clearer, more suitable housing is shown. Every one of these ads from all of these other offices can directly help you and produce the buyer we are looking for.

Incidentally, we are experts at advertising. Not only do we know how to write effective ads, we pay for them."

Had Any Offers? Ask owners if they have had any offers. If the answer is *no*, it reinforces the need for professional help. If *yes*, ask:

"Did you accept it?"

"Why not?"

"Your offer just emphasizes what I have told you about the type of person attracted by For Sale By Owner ads. They either hope to pay less than the property is worth or steal it. These people are not buyers."

The Buyer Pool.

"Every agent has a number of buyers they have been working with for some time. When you have an agent, your property becomes available to this large pool of buyers. There is complete cooperation among brokers so that any agent who has a prospective buyer for your property can show it."

The Trouble With Negotiating. Sellers usually feel uneasy about having to handle negotiations, fearing that they will either accept too little or lose a reasonable deal. You can offer a more reassuring means of communication:

> "Many buyers will not consider making an offer directly to an owner if it is for less than full price. If the buyers feel a price is a little high, they will not buy. They feel cheap haggling with an owner. However, when a third person, an agent, is involved, they are willing to let the agent know what they are thinking. Owners and buyers just can't discuss their concerns. They don't want to hurt anyone's feelings. Objections cannot be overcome unless they are known. When an agent is involved, believe me, owners and buyers alike let us know.
>
> I have sold many homes where a buyer's first reaction was 'I am not interested because . . . ,' or 'If it were not for . . . .' Because buyers don't pull their punches when they talk to an agent, we are able to overcome the objections.
>
> When a buyer does criticize a property, owners often take it personally and react strongly. They don't realize that a common buyer tactic is to strongly criticize a property in the belief it will make an owner more receptive to a very low offer. If an owner appears eager to sell, many buyers will want to take advantage of it by using a take-it-or-leave-it approach. It is understandable for an owner to get mad at a ridiculous offer. Nevertheless, acting as an agent, I have often taken initially ridiculously low offers and worked with the buyers until a fair offer was accepted.
>
> When I sell my own property, I use an agent. I am just like any other owner. I know it is difficult to deal directly."

The House Prisoner. If owners have been trying to sell for any length of time, they need little reminding of the inconvenience they've suffered:

> "Right now you have an ad in the paper and a sign on your front lawn. If you leave the phone or house unattended for just a few minutes, you know that's when a buyer will show up. Your home is holding you captive. You are a prisoner in your own home."

Help With Financing. You might ask the owner,

> "What financing have you been able to arrange?"

While an owner might have been trying for some time to sell his or her home, chances are that he or she has done nothing about financing.

"Owners often lose excellent prospective buyers because they can't provide help in financing. You get much more than a qualified buyer for our fee. You get expertise in every area necessary to successfully complete the sale. Our fee is not paid until the sale is closed and final.

This is a chance for you to sell yourself as an expert. Go over types of financing available at the present time in your area, and the advantages of getting FHA or a savings and loan appraisal now.

Explain that you have some advantages in making sure a financial package will work out as intended:

"Many owners believe they have sold their homes only to find, after taking their property off the market for weeks or even months, that the buyers are unable to obtain financing. Owners tend to be polite. Owners don't find out a buyer's earnings and savings at their first meeting. We are not that polite. We know in advance what a buyer can afford."

The Safety Factor. I personally know of a woman who was attacked by a supposed buyer, and I have been told of similar cases. I believe safety is an important reason to use an agent. I have been criticized for my views by people who claim I am advocating that agents take advantage of the fears of owners. I believe the following approach is based upon the reality of today's urban world. It is not a fear approach but a common sense approach for survival:

"You might not have realized it, but that sign on your front lawn tells the whole world, "Come on in." Besides legitimate buyers and those notorious 'Lookie Loos' you could well attract the wrong kind of person—one interested not in the house but what or who is in it. Thieves know a For Sale By Owner sign is an open invitation for them. Any police officer will tell you that you're asking for trouble by inviting strangers into your home.

>We qualify every prospective buyer we show. We know who
>they are, where they're employed, where they live and usually
>how much money they make and have saved. But, most im-
>portant of all, we would never have anyone enter your home who
>isn't escorted by an agent.
>
>Are you willing to take the risks involved to your family and
>property by letting strangers enter your home?"

This can be one of the strongest Power arguments, and it is
not exaggerated. Agents do offer protection.

WHY US?

When you've sold an owner on using an agent, your next step
is to sell the owner on yourself and your firm as that agent.

Your approach should be coordinated with your presentation book. As you turn the pages, give the reasons why
owners should allow you to represent them. Emphasize your
firm, not yourself, differentiating it from other firms in a
positive fashion. A smooth presentation and your ability to
answer owner questions will generally sell you far better than
self-serving statements about how good you are. This section
describes ways to make your firm's qualities show up in the
most flattering light.

The Small Firm. You can make the fact that your firm is small
into an asset:

>"By specializing in a small number of select properties, we are
>able to provide you with maximum service. Your home will not
>be competing with 300 other office listings. We can provide the
>individual special attention that will mean a successful sale."

If your firm is small, but you belong to a multiple listing
service, you could state:

>"Not only will our own sales staff and advertising help to sell
>your home, but we belong to a multiple listing service of over 300
>brokers and 2,000 salespeople. With Clyde Realty representing
>you, you will be able to take advantage of this huge sales force

and hundreds of thousands of advertising dollars. Our multiple listing service will make your home available to every prospective buyer who contacts any of these agents or offices.''

The Large Firm. If your firm is large, treat that as a benefit to the owners:

> "We offer nine offices and 211 professional salespeople to serve you. Each of these salespeople is probably dealing currently with at least five prospective buyers who are interested in homes in this price range. Letting Allied Realty represent you will mean that tomorrow your home could be exposed to over 1,000 potential buyers.
>
> In the last 12 months our firm has sold 812 homes. What we did for 812 owners we can do for you. Don't you agree that with 812 successes we have proven our ability to sell your home?"
>
> "Salespeople like to sell their own inventory because sales of homes represented by other agents mean a lower selling fee. This is easy to understand. With a small office you, therefore, would have only a handful of agents who are interested in giving a home preferential treatment. In our office you will have 211 salespeople who will be giving your home preferential treatment."

If your office has a large advertising budget, let the owners know about it:

> "Our office spends in excess of $150,000 each year on advertising. That's $3,000 each week. Over the years this advertising has built our name recognition and a following of buyers."

Your membership in a franchise can be a strong reason for sellers to list with you:

> "The fact that we are a member of the World Real Estate Network will help us sell your home. Not only does our national organization provide our office with instant name recognition for buyers entering the community, but our millions of dollars in national advertising has helped us build a strong local following. Our national affiliation provides a referral service from 1,817 offices coast to coast. Buyers relocating from those areas are referred to us and through us to your home."

Referral Service. If your office belongs to a national referral service, let the owners know:

> "Don't you agree that it would be advantageous to get the first chance to sell people moving to our area? We are a member of a 3,000-office national referral service. We are notified of and contacted by families relocating to our community from every state in the nation, thus providing us with special access to very special buyers—very special because they have usually just sold a home elsewhere and are able to make significant down payments or cash purchases."

Specialization. If you or your office specialize in an area or type of property, you have a strong selling point:

> "I am a specialist in motels. In the past 12 months I personally have sold more motel room units than any other office on the south side, and this includes offices with over 300 salespeople."

> "We specialize in Sunny Estates resales. We don't drag our prospective buyers off to other areas."

> "There is a good reason why I have personally represented more owners in the sale of College Heights homes than any other agent. I regard College Heights as my territory. I know every home in the area and every owner. Because I specialize in College Heights, I can serve you better than any other agent."

> "I live at 1814 Kildare Street, only four blocks from here. I know and work this area. Your home could be said to be in my territory."

Statistical Proof of Success. Your actual sales statistics can be effectively used to differentiate your firm from others. Generally the sale-to-listing ratio is not a good ratio to use. Because of market conditions and the tendency of some agents to list anything at any price, these statistics may not look that good. Even when they are good, the ratio will indicate failures. A 68 percent success ratio is also a 32 percent failure ratio.

A better way is to compare the percentage of your listings sold to the average for your multiple listing service. Because a great many of the properties listed are at ridiculous prices, your sales ratio should be significantly higher than the average. By simply taking several hundred listings at random, you can get a fairly accurate percentage for your MLS success rate. If your multiple listing service sells 39 percent of its listings, and your office has a 48 percent sales record, you could accurately state:

> "Our record speaks for itself. Based upon the records of the Buffalo Valley Multiple Listing Service, buyers we represent can expect more than a 20 percent greater likelihood of success than the average reported by the multiple listing service. I don't know of any other office that can claim that kind of success."

The ratio of sale price to original listing price can also be compared with the average reported sale in your multiple listing service:

> "Our listing service reports sale prices of homes sold. In the last ninety days they reported 237 sales. These sales averaged 15 percent below the original asking prices. While not every sale our office made during this period was at the exact list price, our average sale was only 5 percent under the asking price; that's 200 percent better than our competitors. This means we saved owners twice the real estate fees by negotiating higher prices. Isn't this the kind of representation you want?"

The comparison of average time to sell a listing should also seem favorable when compared to a multiple listing service average. Rather than saying your average sale took 58 days compared to an 85-day average, you could state,

> "In representing you we don't delay in finding a qualified buyer. The sales data of the Buffalo Valley Multiple Listing Service shows our success. Our average sale took 27 days less than the average for the entire multiple listing service."

The percent of your sales that are your own listings can also become a strong plus:

> "While there are over 2,000 salespeople in our multiple listing service, 89 percent of our sales are by the agents in our office. We do more than just distribute information about your prop-

erty to a multiple listing service hoping someone else will sell it. We consider ourselves, not others, to be primarily responsible for selling property entrusted to us."

Note that you are not saying that you sell 89 percent of your listings, you are saying that 89 percent of your sales are your own listings. You simply don't sell many listings of other offices. Many firms have similarly high ratios.

Financing Connections. Most offices work with lenders and have developed loan sources. Here are two ways to take advantage of that fact:

> "In this time of tight money, the ability to obtain financing for a buyer can mean the difference between success and failure. Over the years we have developed not only an excellent relationship with lenders, but also many private sources of loans."

> "Don't you agree that you want an agent who can obtain financing for a buyer despite market conditions? Mr. Kotch, our broker, as you probably know, is on the Board of Directors of Villard Loan & Savings."

Emphasize that you are experts in tailoring financing to meet the needs of both buyers and sellers. You should be fully prepared to answer specific questions.

Foreign Buyers. Some offices have relationships with foreign brokers. The buyers referred are usually interested in raw land or farm land, although some are residential buyers. Today many Americans look at foreigners the way foreigners looked at us about thirty years ago. We think they have a lot of money and are waiting to spend it foolishly. If your office has foreign cooperating brokers, explain the benefits that result:

> "An advantage our firm offers is that we are the only local firm which actively solicits foreign buyers. We have a working contractual relationship with three real estate firms in Germany, two in France, one in Italy and we are negotiating with a number of foreign buyers."

Don't underestimate the effectiveness of foreign connections in obtaining listings.

The Guaranteed Sale Plan. If your office has a guaranteed sale or purchase plan, let the owners know:

> "Having Ajax Realty represent you actually guarantees that your home will be sold. If we fail to sell your home within ninety days, we agree in writing to buy the home ourselves at the list price less the commission and 10 percent."

This type of purchase plan was used extensively when good financing was available. The broker guaranteed the sale only after approving the listing, giving the agent additional ammunition for getting good realistically priced listings.

The Home Protection Plan. If your office has a buyers' home protection plan, let the owners know:

> "One of the reasons we attract so many buyers is because we guarantee the homes we sell. Our home protection warranty protects buyers against unexpected home maintenance expense during their first year of ownership. This plan will make your home more desirable than homes offered by other offices."

Proven Honesty. Never tell an owner how honest you are. People who brag about being honest usually are not. If, however, you carry an errors and omissions policy, you have a way to call attention to a good reputation:

> "Fidelity National Insurance Company guarantees the integrity of Allied Realty and all of our agents. After their investigation they have issued a million-dollar policy protecting owners from any wrongful act on our part. It's easy to say you are honest, but words don't mean anything. Fidelity National guarantees our honesty."

About the Competition . . . . In differentiating your firm from others, *never* speak ill of your competition. One successful agent has a stock answer when anyone asks about another firm:

"They are an excellent firm but they do have a problem. Do you know what it is? They don't have me. I am the best sales-person in town and that is no boast. In fact, I am going to prove it to you. You have talked to someone from   Realty haven't you? [Normally the answer will be positive or they would not have asked you about the firm.]   You have not re-tained them to sell your property. The reason is they didn't really sell you on themselves. Now you are going to retain Clyde Realty to represent you because I am going to not only sell you on my firm, but I will sell you on myself. I am also going to find a qualified buyer whom I will sell on your house."

While this approach is too strong for my taste, it works for this salesperson because he exudes confidence.

However you do it, you must demonstrate the advan-tages your firm offers over the competition. If you cannot show owners how your representation will benefit them more than representation by others, you cannot expect to obtain listings in competitive situations.

6

Overcoming Objections

Your presentation has gone a long way toward persuading the owners that they should use an agent to sell their property, and that you are the agent who can best serve their interests. Getting a signature on a listing agreement, however, will not happen until you have brought the owners' objections into the open and overcome them. This chapter points out ways to discover objections, and presents detailed responses to a variety of the objections you will encounter.

Before you can overcome owner objections, you must know what those objections are. The simplest way to find out is simple: ask questions and listen carefully to the answers. Once you feel you've heard and understood the owners' objections (*questions* when you are talking to the owners —*objections* sound too difficult), repeat them back. Ask if these are the only items that concern them. You may have to do this more than once in order to get a clear affirmative answer. When you do, it is time to overcome each objection and go into your closing presentation.

READING BODY LANGUAGE

You may find that what an owner says does not match his or her attitude as you perceive it. Watching body language can give you clues to problems that mere verbal answers conceal. Owners who cross their arms, for example, are often indicating that they need additional selling. They are resisting your sales approach. Perhaps a change of subject is in order: complimenting the owners on decorations, a painting in the home, or other features. You want the owners to open up those arms and accept your presentation.

An owner who crosses and recrosses his or her legs is indicating impatience, as is one who keeps checking a watch. There are two ways to deal with owner impatience: try for a closing now, or set up a definite appointment for a presentation at another time. If you encounter the impatience at the start of your presentation, I recommend you suggest returning at a stated time. If you encounter impatience after you have made most of your presentation, take it as readiness to sign and go for a closing right then.

OBJECTION OR EXCUSE?

Don't let an owner sidetrack you with excuses. Excuses are not reasons. Excuses are raised to avoid or delay decisions. While real objections must be overcome before you can obtain a listing, excuses are merely a smokescreen. Ignore them.

One way to deal with a probable excuse is to say, "I'm glad you brought that up. However, I would like to cover that matter a little later." If it is an excuse, the owner probably will not mention it again. If he or she does, then treat it as an objection and overcome it. Should an owner raise an issue which you feel cannot be overcome, handle it as if it were an excuse: it may well be one.

OBJECTIONS AND RESPONSES

The objections you encounter will each be unique, depending on the owners' personalities and the selling situation. Still, you will find that nearly all of the objections fit into a few dozen basic categories. This section describes the basic objections and gives Power responses to overcome them.

These answers will serve you best if you treat them as exercises: study them until they become second nature to you, and practice using them until you can apply them smoothly and effectively to any variation of the basic objections. When you do this, you will find that the ability to overcome objections becomes a natural pattern which enables you to work spontaneously, concentrating on hearing and understanding your prospects' responses instead of thinking about what you are going to say next.

"I want a new home first." Owners sometimes fear that if they sell their present home without having signed a deal on a new one, they will end up without a roof over their heads. It is your duty to point out the pitfalls of this approach:

> "If you sell your house first, you will be under pressure to sell, and a sale under pressure can mean getting less than market value for your home. It is easier to buy than to sell because in buying you control the transaction. If you were to put in an offer contingent upon selling your house, it is going to be a weak offer and will probably be turned down unless you agree to pay a premium price. You just don't have any bargaining power unless you are able to make a firm offer."

"I don't trust any of you real estate people."

> "I can understand why you feel the way you do. Certainly there have been problems in the past with unethical real estate agents, and you don't really know me. However, I am sure you know of my firm, Shorewood Realty, which has been in business at the same location for 16 years. We could not have stayed in business this long if we didn't treat people fairly."

> "Here is a list of names, addresses and phone numbers of owners I have successfully served. You will notice several are in this

neighborhood. I would like you to call any one of them right now and ask about me and my firm. I feel the people I have worked for are the best people to judge me, don't you agree?''

Chances are the owner will not make a call and the objection will be dropped.

"I know as much about it as you do." Some owners know as much or more about real estate as many professionals. They are usually very successful people in other areas. These people feel they can sell their own property, and they probably can; however, as an agent, you can do a better job. The owners might realize this, but have boxed themselves in telling friends or a spouse how they were going to save a commission. The owners then will resist listing to save face. The following approach can provide an out:

"Mr. Jones, most of the owners I talk to know very little about real estate other than the fact that a house is a place to live in. It is refreshing to find someone not in the business who is as knowledgeable as you are.

The principle advantage that we can offer someone with your knowledge and experience is the greater exposure to qualified buyers possible through our office and our multiple listing service. With enough time, though, I'm sure you could find a buyer on your own. However, consider the fact that my time is not nearly as valuable as yours. Doesn't it make sense to have an agent handle the chore of finding a buyer and completing the sale, so you can use your time more productively?"

This is not a really strong argument, but you have given the "expert" a logical reason to let someone else handle the sale.

"I don't think this is a good time to sell."

"The best time to sell is when you can locate a buyer. I feel we will succeed in this respect. Remember, we are not looking for dozens of buyers. All we need to find is one."

"The market is poor."

> "That's why it is so essential that you obtain professional help. You need the best representation possible."

"I don't need you—there are lots of buyers around."

> "That's just why you need professional help. The market now is good. With professional help you can take advantage of the market and obtain the best possible price and terms. Terms can be as important as price. If you provide any buyer financing, just a half percent difference in the interest rates would more than offset any fee you saved by selling the property yourself."

The owner is really objecting to paying a commission, so continue with the response to the following objection.

"I don't want to pay a commission."

> "Actually it is the buyer who pays the fee. The fee is paid out of the money the buyer puts up. The price the buyer pays includes a fee. The more the buyer pays, the higher the fee. Our interests are identical; we both want to locate a buyer who will pay the highest possible price."

The above is absolutely true. While contractually the owner is obligated, in reality the buyer is the one who pays a price which includes the commission.

> "The buyer sets the price and pays the fee. Some owners feel that if a broker were not involved, then the buyer would pay the fee to them in the form of a higher price. This is not the case. Owners who sell property themselves actually net less money on the average than owners who are represented by agents."

Chapter 5 shows how you can support this statement.

Many real estate people get argumentative when an owner objects to a commission, making statements like, "What professional person do you know who supplies his or her services for free?"

This response alienates the owner by putting him or her down. People don't like to be embarrassed or shown to be wrong. You may be able to brag to your fellow salespeople about how you put the owner in his or her place, but chances are you won't do it with a listing in your hand.

Very often the commission is the real problem underlying other objections and excuses. The owners hope to save money. Therefore, I recommend this objection be overcome even when it is not openly stated.

"Your commission is too high."

"A reduced fee wouldn't really be fair to you. Assume you were a real estate salesperson and you had two homes which met a prospective buyer's needs. One listing allowed a normal fee while the other was at a cut-rate fee. Which home would you try to sell?"

"Our own salespeople would feel this way, but so would salespeople in every other office in the city. That's why when a cut-rate fee is involved the property is seldom sold. If it is sold, it is usually by the salesperson who took the listing. By reducing the fee, you reduce your chances of a sale. You could waste a lot of time and still have an unsold house. Not because buyers wouldn't want it, but rather because salespeople just wouldn't show it to them."

Another approach to the fee question is to go back to the previous approach: the owner is not paying it.

A growing number of brokers list property at reduced fees but expend minimum effort toward consummating a sale. If you are competing against such cut-rate brokers, you need to go on the offensive:

"Cutting fees is a desperate act by brokers who find themselves unable to effectively compete based upon their professional success. Instead of selling you on their ability, they sell the fact that they charge less. These cut-rate brokers are not going to give away more than you are paying for. Reduced fees go hand in hand with reduced effort and reduced chances of success. Actually you are likely to save not just a difference in fees but the entire fee since, with such a broker, your house will likely remain unsold."

"I must sell the property. I can't be tied up with a listing."

"That's exactly why you should list with an exclusive agency agreement to sell your home. Experience has shown that not only does it take owners working alone longer to sell their property, but even when they do accept an offer, they have more than doubled their chances of running into a problem that prevents closing.

"I'm too busy to talk to you."

"This is why I am here: to help you because you are so busy."

"If this is your first meeting with the owners, try to set up a definite appointment to meet with them again. If not, continue with your presentation.

"I have a friend in real estate."

"If you list with a friend, your friend really becomes your employee. Would you hire your friend?"

"What would you do if your friend can't produce a buyer?"

"One problem about doing business with friends is that it is difficult to be objective in dealing with each other. Neither party wants to hurt the other, so honest communication becomes impossible."

"Why haven't you given the listing to your friend? If your friend hasn't sold you on letting him or her represent you, is your friend going to be able to persuade a buyer to sign an offer and put down a deposit?"

"You could lose a friend by mixing business and friendship. Would you hesitate to let me know if you're not happy with the job I'm doing? I know I'll be hearing from you if I don't produce. But what if I were your friend?"

"Suppose your friend brought you a poor offer, and he or she wanted you to accept it in order to earn a fee. What do you do?

Do you accept the offer and hurt yourself or refuse and hurt your friendship? Because you have a friend in the business is the reason why I should represent you—so you can retain the friendship."

Most salespeople use the classic:

"That's great. We are members of the multiple listing service and cooperate with all licensed agents; therefore your friend can earn a fee by selling the property."

If the owner indicates he or she has promised the friend the listing, this is a Power approach:

"I am surprised that your friend was willing to wait. I hope your friend isn't willing to wait when he or she has a hot prospect. This is my business and I am successful at it because of my philosophy—do it now. Do you feel this friend will do a better job in dealing with buyers than I would?"

"We are really talking business, not friendship. You must do what is best for *you*."

If the conversation reveals that the owner's friend works part time in real estate,

"I work full time and am willing to devote my full efforts to sell your home. Would you be satisfied with a part-time effort?"

"I don't take a listing in the hope of someone else selling it and earning a fee for me. My primary responsibility is to see that my listings are sold. I don't sit back and hope someone else will do the job for me."

The friend may turn out to be just an excuse. After you have given your response to the friend objection, continue with your presentation.

"I would like to talk to the people at Acme Realty first."

"Is there any information Acme Realty can give you that I haven't provided?"

"What do you think Acme Realty can do that I can't do?"

"I don't need you—I already have a buyer."

> "That's great. Has your buyer signed a contract yet and given you a down payment?"

Normally the answer will be no, but if it is yes, ask to see the contract. Offer to help the owner. Read the contract for problems. If you find any, suggest clarifications or even getting legal advice. You should take an interested, helpful approach.

Owner sales often fail because the buyers have not been qualified. Ask the owners about the buyers and whether they have been qualified and credit checked. The answer will undoubtedly be no. Tell the owners you hope it turns out all right, but if there are any problems, or if they need advice, to call you and you will try to help them. These few minutes can well mean a listing, as a high percentage of direct owner sales are never completed.

More likely, you'll find that the buyers have not signed a contract or given a deposit "yet." This is an opportunity to make an irresistible proposition:

> "Mr. and Mrs. Schmidley, I am going to help you sell your home to your buyers, and it isn't going to cost you one cent. What I suggest is that you agree to let Classic Realty represent you with an exclusion. If your buyers will contract to buy your home within 10 days, our agency agreement will be cancelled with absolutely no cost to you.
>
> What this will do is force your buyers to act. Your buyers will realize that after the 10 days they will have to pay a fee. If the buyers are ever going to buy, you can see this will force them to act now. Some people are really not able to buy, but keep owners on edge for months while they wait for some help or some miracle which never comes along. This approach will save you a lot of time and possible aggravation. Does this approach make sense to you?"

If the owners agree that the approach makes sense, they are really agreeing to a listing, which should now be presented for signature.

Chapter 7 explains a similar approach for situations where the owners say they have a prospect or even several prospects.

7

The Realistic Listing

You've worked hard to learn how to find sellers, make an effective presentation, and overcome objections. It seems only right that having gotten this far, you can at last jump into the closing and get on with the business of selling the property. But take a moment to stop and ask whether the listing you are about to get will be salable. Is the price competitive? Are the terms attractive? Does the arrangement offer *you* enough to bring out your honest best effort?

Unless you can answer those questions with a definite *yes*, you have one further challenge to meet before the closing: you must persuade the owners not just to give you a listing, but to develop a realistic listing that will be in the best interests of themselves, you, and everyone else concerned. This chapter shows you what to look for in terms of seller motivation, when to turn down a listing, and how to explain to sellers that they must make their property package realistic enough to bring in serious offers.

ASSESSING MOTIVATION

Your efforts to obtain listings should relate directly to the owner's motivation. Your greatest effort should be directed toward Must Sell rather than Will Sell situations. Will Sell listings usually mean unrealistic prices and terms and a long, perhaps unsuccessful, sales effort.

Motivating the Hesitant Seller. Often owners are considering selling but have no real motivation. They can afford more expensive housing but don't feel a strong desire for it. They may not view themselves as the kind of people who live in luxurious homes.

It has been said that we would still be living in caves were it not for the first real estate salesperson who sold the first log hut. People often don't fully realize what they want until they see what they don't have.

While in high school, I sold clothing in a department store. Often men who were waiting for their wives would wander over to our department. If we could get a suit coat off the rack and on their backs and get them in front of a mirror, we could create a desire to own that suit. The same principle applies to real estate sales. People don't seriously want something until they see what they can have. Half a day spent showing available homes to a couple living in more modest surroundings can turn "just thinking about it" owners into motivated sellers, which can mean a realistic listing. Seeing what is within their reach often pushes the right emotional button to make a better home an urgent necessity.

Here is a way to set up such a showing:

"I wouldn't want you to sell your home and then find yourselves in a situation where suitable housing was not available. Before you make any decision, I would like you to spend just a few

hours with me looking at available housing within an acceptable
price range."

WHEN NOT TO TAKE A LISTING

While there are many reasons brokers fail, I believe the desire
to build up an inventory without caring about quality ranks
among the top three. No matter how great the quantity of
listings, without quality, success will elude the broker. A top
investment property salesman who recently left a large firm
told me that the firm had over 100 investment listings
totaling over 25 million dollars, but not one listing that was
not overpriced—and their sales reflected it.

Being offered a listing doesn't always mean you should
take it. Good listings are the key to success, but bad listings
are worse than nothing. They waste time and advertising
dollars to start with, and eventually drive away serious
buyers who get tired of being shown overpriced and unsuit-
able property.

Since overpriced listings seldom sell, they create ill will
with the owner and harm your firm's reputation. Listings
that expire unsold advertise your failure, finally decreasing
your ability to obtain quality listings in your area. The more
marginal listings you take, the lower your chances of success become.

Leave the Crumbs. It is indeed possible that a listing you turn
down will be taken by another agent. It is even possible that
the property will sell at its listed price. Though you kick
yourself for having turned down that particular listing, in the
long run you will be far ahead. A real estate salesperson
needs optimism, but there is a difference between the practical optimist and the Pollyanna escaping from reality.

The Honest Price. Don't take an overpriced listing with the secret
intent of "working down" the owner. You are better off
refusing the listing. If the owner lists with another broker
at an unrealistic price, you will be in a strong position to
obtain the listing when it expires unsold.

Stay With What You Know. Listings outside your experience or
geographical area should be refused. If you have only sold
single-family homes, don't list a factory. If you cannot
adequately service the listing with an expectation of success,
don't take it. Ethics require a commitment to diligently
seek consummation of a sale. Where diligence is not possible,
you cannot honestly make such a commitment.

Listings you cannot handle well mean aggravation and
ill will. Referring such listings to a broker who can adequately meet their needs will enhance your reputation, and could
earn you a referral fee.

POWER PATHS TO APPROPRIATE PRICES

Many real estate salespeople take poor listings even though
they have motivated owners. Agreeing with everything an
owner wants is not helping the owner—you have a duty to
say no to unrealistic prices and terms, and to support your
position with facts. A real estate agent represents the owner's
best interest and going along with an unrealistic price or
conditions is *not* in the owner's best interest. The owner's
best interest calls for a listing that will attract qualified
buyers.

You have a duty to be persuasive even when the per-
suasion is directed at your principals, the owners. You must
strive for a realistic listing as well as for acceptance of a
realistic offer.

The duty to help owners find a realistic price works for
low prices as well as high ones. Suggesting or accepting a
lower price than you expect the property to sell for is repre-
hensible conduct. It violates the fiduciary duty of financial
trust which a real estate licensee has to the owner. In the
long run you will find that placing the interests of your
principal above your own interests is to your own benefit.

Don't accept what owners say at face value. If owners
declare that they will not list their property for less than a
particular dollar amount, it usually means merely that they
would love to get that price. The owners are trying to sell
you on their price, while you are trying to sell them on yours.

If you feel that their price is not realistic, continue to strive for a realistically-priced listing.

If owners say they must get a certain price for their home, find out why they feel this need. Understanding an owner's reasoning will enable you to demonstrate the necessity for a realistic listing. The task of changing an owner's expectations can be a difficult one: you must break through long-held emotional beliefs and financial fantasies. Fortunately, reason and reality are strong tools for change when used correctly. The following techniques and arguments have proven their effectiveness in getting owners to begin thinking more realistically.

Overpriced Sales Don't Close. An owner may believe that if he or she can just get a buyer at the overpriced listing figure, everything will be fine. You'll do best by shattering that myth early in the game:

> "Let's assume for a moment that we list the property at the price you suggest of $_____. Assume further that I am able to find a buyer at the price listed. The sale probably would never be consummated. Lenders make loans based on appraisals of market value, not what one particular buyer might be willing to pay. From my comparables we know the market value. The appraiser has the same information we have. What do you suppose will happen when the lender tells the buyers that the price they are offering is in excess of the real value of the property?"

The Appraiser Gamble. One of my students told me how a broker effectively used a Power approach to get her to reduce her list price. My student did not feel that the price she wanted was out of line.

Her broker asked to see a phone book and turned to Real Estate Appraisals in the Yellow Pages. He then said:

> "Are you a gambler? Pick any appraiser with either the MAI or SREA designation in the ad and order a fee appraisal of your home. If my estimate of $_____ is closer to the appraisal than yours, then you pay the appraisal fee. If, however, you are closer, I will pay the fee and use my best efforts to sell the property at your price."

This proposal convinced the owner that the broker was sincere and not just trying to make his sale easier at her expense. She agreed to the broker's price without an appraisal and her home was sold.

How Would You Feel? You should have completed a competitive market analysis on the property. After going through the analysis, the following Power approach brings home the risk of starting with an overpriced listing:

> "Assume for a moment that you are a buyer and you ask me to prepare a competitive market analysis such as I have just shown you. How would you react to a list price for the home at [owner's address] of $[owner's price]?"
>
> "Buyers prefer to start with sellers who are reasonable. They don't even bother looking at property they feel is not competitively priced."

Owners usually know when another agent has quoted too high a price, but they'd like to believe it anyway. You must get owners back to earth. Your competitive market analysis helps with the re-entry.

Old Listings Tell the Story. Expired and sold listings dramatically illustrate that realistically priced listings sell and overpriced listings expire. One broker made an extremely good Power presentation to me by the use of old listings.

He went through listing sheets of comparable properties, placing them in two piles. One of sold listings and the other of expired listings. All had either sold or expired within six months. On each of the sold listings he had written with a colored marker the number of days it took to sell it.

He then handed me a sheet of paper with two columns corresponding to the two piles of listings. In one column were the addresses and list prices of all the expired listings; in the other, the address, list price, actual sale price and days to sell of the sold listings.

The summary sheet showed very clearly that expired listings had much higher initial prices than the sold listings. Further, the lower the list price, the quicker the property sold.   Most striking of all, the list showed actual sold prices not much different within the range, whether the initial listing had started out high or not.   Homes listed at the lowest prices sold at or very near list price, while homes initially priced higher sold at large discounts after a longer time on the market.

This technique dramatically demonstrates two vital truths: it isn't necessary to overprice a home "because the buyer will offer less," and the only important price in listings of comparable property is the *selling* price, not the list price. The broker played straight with me: he used the listings on every home in my area which I knew had been sold.   He finished by pushing both piles of listings toward me and asking,

"Which pile should we put your listing in?"

Graphic Story I: Price and Probability. Similar facts can also be presented effectively by means of graphs.   The diagram on the next page was prepared by a broker who analyzed her expired and sold listings over a period of several months. She used her competitive market analysis as the basis for market value.   The chart is part of her listing presentation book.   It has proved to be an effective tool for obtaining competitive listings.

While this chart was prepared for a particular area over a particular period of time, you will find similar relationships in your own listings' performances.   Using this chart will help you get competitive listings based on what other properties sell for, rather than what they list at.   This chart illustrates to the owner the advantage of competitive and even slightly below-market listings.

Graphic Story II: Price and Time. Owners usually want a timely sale.   The chart on page 146 shows the relationship of list price to time on market.   Clearly, the more realistic the actual list price, the faster a sale can be expected.

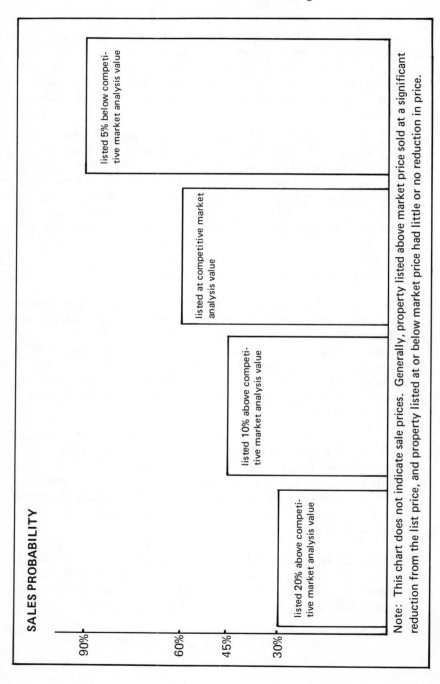

SALES PROBABILITY

90%

60%

45%

30%

listed 5% below competi-
tive market analysis value

listed at competitive market
analysis value

listed 10% above competi-
tive market analysis value

listed 20% above competi-
tive market analysis value

Note: This chart does not indicate sale prices. Generally, property listed above market price sold at a significant reduction from the list price, and property listed at or below market price had little or no reduction in price.

Your own Competitive Market Analysis, actual list prices and the time properties took to sell are the data you need to prepare a similar graph. Your results will probably be much the same as the ones shown.

Testing the Market. If a motivated owner insists on a slightly high listing price, you can take the listing but inform the owner that you will test the price on the market and come back to discuss your results. Get the opinions, in writing, of other agents in your office who viewed the property, as well as agents who show or caravan the home. Ask prospects who viewed the property why they were not interested. Include lender or FHA appraisals. Present all this information to your owners, showing the consensus results of those who saw the property.

Your test results should give you the means to persuade the owners to adjust their list price. Never ask them to "lower" a price. "Lowering" suggests losing something. "Adjusting" means simply setting a more realistic price. While agreeing to honestly test a price is ethical, taking an overpriced listing with the intent of working the owner down isn't.

Returning the Listing. Should an owner resist a price adjustment after you have presented information indicating that the listing price is not realistic, return the listing to the owner and ask to be relieved of your obligations. This Power approach indicates to the owner that you are serious about the need for a price adjustment.

This very powerful presentation makes the point without mincing words:

> "From the analysis I have presented it is clear to me that we were overly optimistic in setting the list price. If we are to be successful in selling your home, I believe an adjustment of $_____ will be necessary, making the sale price $_____.
>
> Since I have been unable to convince you to make this adjustment, the only fair thing would be for me to return our agency agreement and ask that you relieve us of our obligation to secure a buyer for you."

The relationship of average time to sell and list price (market value was the price indicated by our Competitive Market Analysis). Note: This graph was prepared based only on properties which were actually sold. The actual sale price of property listed above market value was usually much less than the list price.

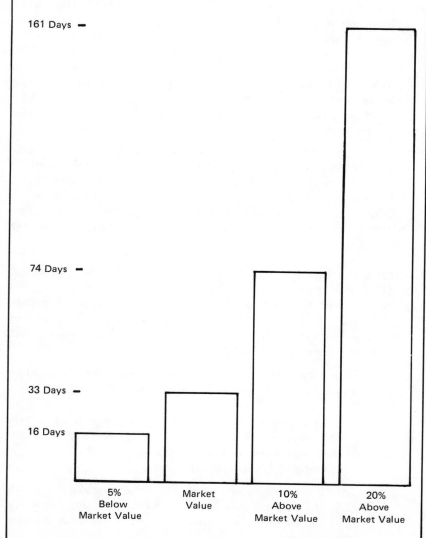

161 Days —

74 Days —

33 Days —

16 Days

5%	Market	10%	20%
Below	Value	Above	Above
Market Value		Market Value	Market Value

Set the listing down before you on the table.

> "It would be deceiving you to let you believe that a sale is likely as listed. If we are to secure a buyer we must be competitive.
>
> Do you really want to sell your house?"

You can expect a positive reaction.

> "Then let's set the price so that we can get it sold."

You can now change the price on the listing and ask the owner to initial and date the change.

Don't Knock the House. Whichever technique you use in trying for a more realistic listing, don't knock the house. You can knock the economy or the financing, but not the house. You must be enthusiastic about the house. Never say that the house is not worth a particular amount. Instead, "The present market won't support that price."

POWER RESPONSES TO OWNER DEMANDS

While you try to sell owners on setting a sensible listing price, they will be trying just as hard to sell you on a higher figure. Owners often believe that if they can sell the real estate agent on their price and terms, the agent will in turn be able to sell prospective buyers. Most owners have no sense of the market: they base their demands on what they honestly feel the property is worth, or on what they feel they deserve to get for it. Following are the major arguments owners use to justify a high price or unreasonable terms, and techniques you can use to get better listings without alienating owners.

"We put $110,000 into this house." Because owners place so much importance on persuading you of the house's value, they sometimes quote fictitious prices that they or their neighbors paid for their properties. Even when you know that the figures are false, you should never confront the owners with their fibs. You must allow them to save face:

"Unfortunately, what owners have invested in a home does not determine its value. What a person wants doesn't determine its value. Buyers determine value. What a qualified buyer is willing to pay is the value. By my comparables, I believe I have shown you what we can realistically expect a qualified buyer to pay."

If owners say that they have more invested in a property than you feel it is worth, determine what they paid for the property. Owners often consider their maintenance and repair costs as what they have "put into it." You will have to explain:

"Repair and maintenance expenses are necessary for all property. These expenditures maintain the value by keeping up the property; they do not increase the value. If you had failed to take the kind of care you have taken, then prospective buyers would reduce their offers by the cost of making repairs."

"I'd be taking a loss at that price." When owners have owned property for a number of years it will generally be worth considerably more than they paid for it. However, at times buyers must actually suffer a loss if they wish to sell. One way to deal with this situation is to downplay the loss:

"Mr. and Mrs. Schmidt, how long have you owned your home?"

"You have had the enjoyment and use of this home for 12 years. Based on comparables, your home is worth $6,000 less than you paid for it. That's only $500 per year [or about $45 a month]. Don't you feel that you have received far more than $500 per year value out of living in this home? I think this home has served you well."

This approach makes a loss seem like a positive benefit because it is so low. This is necessary as owners otherwise are often unwilling to list or sell at figures which will mean a loss.

"We put $20,000 worth of improvements into this house." Owners often overimprove property to the point where they cannot sell at a price that will pay back their investment. A $10,000 swimming pool added in California might increase the total property by $10,000 or even more, but the same pool added in Illinois might increase the value by only $6,000.

Similarly, a $500,000 home in an area of $80,000 homes will not return the owner's investment. Lower-priced homes pull the value down. This is known as the principle of regression. You can explain this to an owner in a positive fashion:

> "Your home is one of the nicest in the neighborhood. Because you have one of the finest homes in the area, the value of your home reflects on your neighbors. Your home actually makes other homes in the area more valuable. Unfortunately, it works both ways. The lower-priced homes of your neighbors tend to pull down the value of your home. If you want to have the best, you must expect to have the value of lesser homes reflect on any sales price."

"We can always reduce the price later." Owners hate to give up their fantasies of making a killing by selling at an outrageous price, so they try to postpone reality by convincing you to start with a high price, then coming down if there are no takers. Once again, your best reply is to point out that the market does not work that way:

> "If a property is realistically priced, other salespeople will be enthusiastic about it. If they are enthusiastic, this will not only be reflected in the level of effort they expend on the property, but their positive attitude will be conveyed to prospective buyers. By overpricing your home, you are really excluding a great many potential buyers. Even though you could be willing to come down to a buyer's price range, the buyer doesn't know that. Potential buyers will ignore ads for homes which they feel are priced beyond their means. If they call about an unpriced ad or a sign, they will not be interested when the price is quoted, so they'll hang up. Other salespeople might use your home to sell other homes. Salespeople often use a home which they consider overpriced to make a realistically priced home appear to be a bargain.
>
> Even though you later reduce the price, a price adjustment is not greeted with the kind of fresh response that greets a new, realistically priced listing. When an overpriced property finally has its

price adjusted to a realistic figure, it will probably have been on the market for some time. Prospective buyers are often leery of old listings. They wonder what's wrong with the property. On the other hand, nothing excites buyers as much as realistically priced new listings."

"When an overpriced listing has been on the market for some time, other brokers are likely to indicate to prospective buyers that they believe the price is 'soft.' If an offer results, it will usually not be just below the list price, it will likely be in the bargain basement price range."

One Power approach is to show owners a mock listing of their home with a Polaroid photo, along with actual listings of comparable homes:

"Imagine yourself as a buyer. Assume you have to choose a home from these photos only. Would you want to see this home if it were priced at $8,000 more than the competing homes? This is our competition. We must actually compete with 400 other homes offered for sale right now. If we don't appear competitive, buyers will not even look at your home, and the chances are we won't be successful."

"He says . . . ." An argument used by some owners is, "My [banker, brother, cousin or friend] told me that I shouldn't list my home for less than $100,000."

Your response to such a statement goes back again to the idea of market value:

"I believe I have demonstrated to you what the market value of your home is. If we were to list your home at the $100,000 that your cousin suggested, we can expect that the list price will discourage some otherwise qualified buyers. If we lose a qualified buyer because we have listed the property at too high a price, will your cousin be willing to buy the property at its fair value?"

This statement points out to the owners that they are the ones that suffer if the listing price discourages buyers. The decision belongs to the owners alone.

"I'll rent it before I sell at that price." When owners say they will rent before they sell at the price you have suggested, point out the risks involved:

> "I am sure you will be able to rent your beautiful home, but renting it now is likely to make it a great deal more difficult to sell when you want to sell, unless you are willing to spend a great deal of money. At best, renters won't give your home the kind of care you have given it. Renters tend to perform minimum maintenance or none at all, and that's with a good tenant. Besides the bother of tenant complaints, rent collection and vacancy problems, you face the possibility of tenants who will leave your property in shambles. I don't believe you want to subject your beautiful home to that kind of risk."

Point out that renters often fail to care for landscaping as well as the interior of the home. Since it isn't their property, renters can't be expected to care for it as the owners have. Renters also call in the middle of the night, break leases or must be evicted.

I recommend you use an actual horror story about renting to which the owners can relate. If you don't know of any, ask your broker or someone in property management.

A story I used actually happened to me. When I left the state, I rented a home on a one-year lease to a professional couple with a high income. They had good credit ratings, which usually goes hand-in-hand with the way people treat property. This time it didn't work that way. Besides letting all my roses die for lack of water, they turned the lawn into a muddy parking lot, wrecked the air conditioner and furnace by running them without filters, and never even used a vacuum cleaner on the carpeting. It took several thousand dollars and weeks of my labor to prepare the house for resale. This sorry tale has persuaded more than one owner to sell rather than rent.

GETTING BETTER TERMS

If an owner will not reduce the list price, there are other ways to make the listing competitive. Agreeing to pay lender points, setting a low down payment or carrying back a mortgage at below the market rate can all help.

Alternatives to Cash. Sellers often insist that they must have cash. Ask them why. Many sellers who want cash really don't need it. There are alternatives to the cash sale. Putting a second mortgage on the property prior to sale could meet the sellers' financial needs.

If the sellers only want the cash to buy another property, show other listings in which the owners will provide financing. If your owners can buy without a great deal of cash, then they can sell in the same manner.

If you feel a seller does not really need the cash, consider the following approach:

"Mr. Lewis, when you purchased your home in 1962 with a VA loan, how much of a down payment did you make?"

Chances are that the owner made a much smaller down payment than would be needed today to get a new loan which would cash out the owner. Point out this reality:

"Mr. Lewis, buyers today are much like you when you purchased this home. You were probably just starting out and didn't have a great deal of money to pay down. Neither do most young families today. You would probably be renting today if you had not been afforded the opportunity to buy with a reasonable down payment."

To illustrate the problem young buyers have today during a high interest period, spell out the financial implications:

"Mr. Lewis, you want $100,000 for your home. To obtain conventional financing, a buyer would need at least 20% down, or $20,000. Financing the balance at 15% interest would mean a monthly payment of $1,024.67, not including taxes or insurance. If we were to apply the general rule that people should not make mortgage payments of more than 25% of their income, then a purchaser would need a monthly income of $4,098.68, or about $50,000 per year. Frankly, Mr. Lewis, I don't believe we will find a young buyer earning $50,000 a year who can pay $20,000 down and make monthly mortgage payments of over $1,000 plus taxes and insurance for your home. Don't you agree that this will be very difficult?"

The above is a Power approach because the present owners probably could not qualify to buy their own home. Because of inflation they have a home which is more valuable than their income could justify if they were the purchasers. This approach naturally leads into the possibility of owner financing.

Selling Owner Financing. In many cases owners will have to help finance buyers if there is to be a sale. Don't try to sell an owner on financing as something that must be done. This is a negative approach. Instead, sell the benefits:

"Mr. Lewis, the present tight money market offers you an exceptional opportunity. You currently owe $45,000 on your home at 6 percent interest. This is a below-market assumable loan that can benefit you. Just for a moment, imagine we found a buyer for $100,000 with a $10,000 down payment who was willing to buy your home if you would handle the financing at 12 percent interest. At first glance, 12 percent doesn't look great because it is below the current market interest rate of about 15 percent. However, the 12 percent rate would apply to the entire $90,000 balance, not just your $45,000 equity. If the buyer were to pay you for $90,000 at 12 percent and you were to make the payments on your $45,000 loan at 6 percent, then you would make a 6 percent interest differential on your existing loan plus 12 percent interest on your equity. What it means is that you will really receive 18% interest on your equity. This type of interest would not be possible on any other secured investment. Does 18 percent secured interest interest you?"

For clarity you should write it out for the owners. The above example could be written out as follows:

Price:	$100,000
— You owe:	45,000
Your equity:	55,000
— Down payment:	10,000
Balance due you:	$ 45,000

You get 12% on $90,000:
>   12% on your $45,000 equity
>   6% on remainder of price $45,000 (you pay 6% on your loan but receive 12%).
You get 18% return on your $45,000

Another advantage of owner financing that you can point out is that the owner will avoid prepayment penalties on existing loans.

For a discussion of a variety of creative financing techniques, see my *Get Rich on Other People's Money* (Arco, 1981).

Using Buydowns to Compete.   If an owner insists on an all-cash sale, show listings of comparable property where the owners offer financing at below-market rates.   This is the competition.   In order to be competitive, the owner must either meet the terms which others offer or agree to a below-market price.

As an alternative to a price adjustment, the owner could agree to "buy down" the interest rate.   Conventional lenders will agree to lend at a below-market rate in exchange for an advance payment.   Check with local lenders to find out what they require for each one percent reduction in interest on a five-year renegotiable loan.

Five years is probably adequate, after which the buyer will refinance at the then-current interest rate.   If the current interest rate is 15%, agreeing to buy down the interest rate to 11% or 12% would make the property interesting to a buyer.   It might well result in a lower cost to the owner than adjusting the price low enough to lure cash buyers or buyers willing to pay current interest rates.

Personal Property: Asset or Liability?   Often owners insist on little things that could just make the difference between a sale and no sale.   Owners might want the buyer to buy their fireplace equipment and drapes, for example.   You should explain that while their request and prices are reasonable, these minor points could muddy up a sale.

"Buyers who intend to redecorate may resist buying the drapes, and a buyer might already have fireplace equipment.   If, like most buyers, they are considering several homes, they are likely to ignore this one because of the hassle over personal property. You are better off to give it to the buyer than to charge for it. This then becomes an inducement to the buyer rather than a problem. The sale price, if necessary, can reflect your decision."

Owners will at times want to sell their homes furnished. Explain that limiting buyers to those interested in a furnished home will significantly reduce the market, since most people either have their own furniture or would like to do their own decorating. You might suggest two prices, one for furnished and one for unfurnished. If the house is sold unfurnished, the furniture can be readily disposed of either to a dealer or through a local classified advertisement. If the owners are in a significant tax bracket, they could come out ahead by giving the furniture away. A donation of furniture to the Salvation Army or other groups will not only help the charity, but can provide a tax deduction based on what a dealer would sell (not buy) the furniture for. The tax advantages can actually be greater in net benefits than would selling the furniture with the house or to a dealer.

THE LISTING FOR YOU

You can do your job well only when the terms of the listing benefit rather than hinder you. A realistic listing must be fair to you, as well as the seller and buyer. Here are some points to watch for, and methods for getting what you need.

Expanding the Short-Term Listing. A short listing period works against the owners' best interest. A quick expiration date does not lead to a quick sale—it usually ensures that the property will not be sold. Often owners insist on a 30-day listing period after they have tried unsuccessfully to sell the property on their own. This is a very effective Power approach for handling that situation:

"Mr. Perkins, how long have you been trying to sell your home?"

"Do you think it is fair now to give me only 30 days?"

"It takes time to sell. First of all, information on your home must be printed and distributed to our own salespeople and salespeople in other offices. We must arrange to show the property to these salespeople. Lenders must be contacted for financing and lender appraisals. Advertising must be prepared and sent to the various media, and now we are just getting ready for buyers.

Few buyers buy a home like a suit of clothes. Buyers take their time because they are probably making the biggest investment of their lives. If often takes multiple showings and comparisons before an offer is forthcoming. Even then we might have counter-offers and even counters to the counteroffers. No, 30 days is just not enough time."

You can point out that studies have shown that the longer the listing period the greater is the likelihood of a sale. Check with your local board of Realtors ® for the average time it takes for a sale. It may be over two months, depending upon the economy.

An extremely persuasive argument has been used for many years. I don't know who originated it, but I first heard it at a seminar in the 1950s. It goes like this:

"Most sales are made on weekends; that gives us eight good selling days each month if the weather permits. Now this weekend will be lost, as we are too late to meet the advertising deadline and get the information distributed to all the real estate offices in time. That leaves just three weekends or six working days to sell your home, and that's providing it doesn't rain. Do you feel that giving me six days is sufficient? I don't think so."

A final approach to getting a reasonable listing period has strong shock value:

"Well if that is all the time you will allow us, we can do it. You could reduce the price another $20,000 and change the listing to $80,000."

The owner will get very agitated at this suggestion. You can now explain:

"I guess I misunderstood you. I thought you had to sell within 30 days. That to me means an auction-type sale. To find buyers who will jump to buy quickly, we must have an auction-type price. If you are willing to give a bargain price, I can sell it fast; but if you want reasonable value, I need a reasonable period of time to sell."

Exclusive Right-to-Sell Listings. In real estate you don't really have control over buyers. What you do control is the property that makes up your inventory. You control your property through exclusive right-to-sell listings. If any of your inventory is sold by anyone during the term of its listing, you have earned yourself a commission.

As far as you are concerned, this should be the only kind of listing there is. Don't even mention other types of listings to an owner. An exclusive right-to-sell listing is the only listing that provides an owner with the professional assistance he or she needs.

Verbal Listings. Some brokers will work on "Vest Pocket Listings." These are verbal listings which are no listings at all. These brokers know of an owner who will sell and has verbally promised to pay a commission. A verbal listing is an invitation to work for free. I have had owners tell me, "My word is my bond." Personally, I have yet to meet an honest person who considered it necessary to advertise his or her honesty. If people are truly honest, they will not object to putting an agreement in writing. A signed agreement protects the owner as well as the broker. Without an agreement, neither is obligated to perform.

Open Listings. Open listings are nonexclusive listings which might be given out to a number of brokers. Most real estate brokers who take open listings have been unable to compete effectively for exclusive right-to-sell listings. Because they lack a controlled inventory, they will work on open listings.

Don't waste your time on a listing which can mean no commission if sold by another office or by the owners themselves. Open listings are just one step above no listing at all.

A Chinese proverb says, "A pig with two masters will surely starve." Unless someone is responsible for a sale it won't happen. An expression that even better describes open listings is originally credited to Izaak Walton: "Everybody's business is nobody's business."

Exclusive Agency Listings. It isn't necessary to take an exclusive agency listing. With this, you earn a commission if you or any other agent sells the property, but not if the owners sell the property themselves. With this type of listing, the owner really isn't on your team. Owners will work around you to avoid paying a commission. Listings must involve trust; the exclusive agency listings promulgate distrust.

Owners usually want this type of listing because they think they may have a buyer. They don't want to pay you for selling to the buyer they found. This is a reasonable feeling, and you can use it to get an exclusive right-to-sell listing.

The following is a slight variation of the approach discussed in Chapter 5:

> "I can understand your position, Mr. Johnson. I would not want you to be obligated to my firm if one of the buyers you have found buys your home. I am willing to help you sell to one of these buyers and it will not cost you one cent. What we will do is write an exclusive right-to-sell agreement with an exclusion for your buyers, whom we will name. This exclusion will be for one week. If any of these buyers is truly serious, they will buy now, knowing that delay will cost them a fee. If they are serious and have any intention of buying, we will force them to act. If they don't buy, you will know they were just "lookers" who spend time, not money."

You will either help the owners sell their property or have an exclusive right-to-sell listing after one week, as well as a few new prospective buyers.

Net Listings. Under a net listing the broker gets everything over a net sale price as a commission. This looks great, but don't take one. Net listings are trouble. To start with, they create ethical problems. The broker's interests are no longer the same as the owner's. The broker is no longer a true agent.

From a practical viewpoint, should a buyer offer the list price or less, you will have worked for free; but should you make an extraordinary profit, you can expect a lawsuit claiming fraud and breach of fiduciary duty in recommending too low a price and a net listing.

Net listings are illegal in at least one state and subject to stringent regulations in others.

Listings Combined With Options. Land brokers formerly took listings combined with options to buy. A broker might list a parcel of raw land for $10,000 with a 10 percent commission, for example. The broker then offers the owner $50 for the option to buy the property for $9,000 without any commission being paid. Since the owner would net the same on either sale, the $50 looks like found money to the owner.

The broker now has a free hand. If an offer comes in for $8,000, the broker could handle it under the listing to earn an $800 commission. If, however, a prospect offers $14,000, the broker can exercise the option, buy the property for $9,000, resell it for $14,000, and make a $5,000 profit.

Like the net listing, a listing combined with an option is an invitation to a lawsuit. In addition, many states strictly regulate or prohibit this type of activity.

Exclusive right-to-sell listings offer all the opportunity to make money any ethical salesperson could want. Playing the tricky listing game reflects not only on your own character, but upon all real estate professionals. It is to be avoided by you and condemned in others.

8
The Closing and After

Everything you have said and done so far has been aimed at the moment of truth—when the owners sign the listing agreement. This chapter shows you how to reach that point through Power closing strategies, then gives points on how to make the most of the listing once you've gotten it.

POWER CLOSING STRATEGIES

Once you've gotten this far, you know the owners are strongly leaning in the direction of giving you their listing. Otherwise they would not have let you spend so much time with them. Closing a listing, then, is simply a way of harvesting all the good will and awareness of benefits that you have sown in your dealings with the owners.

The Right Words. Owners about to sell their house are usually very nervous, so it is important to use language that maintains the awareness of potential benefits that you have worked to instill. Certain words create a negative response in most people, aggravating the natural fear and anxiety that go with making such a major decision.

Asking for a *listing* is one such statement. What you really want is to represent the owners, to have them "approve an agency agreement," or to "authorize you to represent them." Representation is a benefit. Benefits are easy to sell. A listing, on the other hand, brings to mind the commission, something that costs money. Whenever possible, avoid the term "listing" altogether. Keep the focus on the benefits, not the costs.

The *contract* is another term that scares most people. A contract is simply a binding agreement, so use the term *agreement* to avoid the negative emotional associations that contracts can have. The same uneasiness is triggered by the prospect of *signing* things. Everyone has heard warnings about signing their names to contracts. Most people are perfectly happy to *approve* what they have agreed to, however, so ask owners to "approve our agreement."

Another negative association goes with the word *commission*. People try to avoid commissions, but expect to pay *fees* for professional services. Use that term.

The Summation. When all objections have been overcome and all differences resolved, it is time to go for the listing. Just as a courtroom lawyer gives a summation to the jury covering all his major points and showing how they lead to the right decision, you should give a summation of the major thrust of your presentation, pointing out the benefits of a correct decision.

Keep in mind that owners want to sell but need assurances that letting you represent them is in their best interest. Your summation should meet that need:

"Mr. and Mrs. Thomas, I would like to summarize our discussion. I have shown you that my firm specializes in this area and that we have an exceptional success rate. We not only know the housing market, but we have numerous sources and methods of financing which can be tailored to best meet your needs as well as the needs of buyers.

I have shown you why most buyers prefer to deal through brokers and that having your own agent representing you will mean the highest net and most advantageous terms for you. I have also explained the legal problems often associated with direct owner sales.

Of great importance today is the security aspect of a sale. We know the people we bring to your home, and we've checked their backgrounds. We don't bring in strangers off the street who could want entrance to your home for reasons other than buying it."

If the seller is being transferred from the area, you could continue:

"Probably the most important benefit of employing me as your representative will be to avoid delays. Since you must be in Denver by June 1, the inability to conclude a sale in a reasonable period of time could mean your family would be separated, which, as you realize, could subject them to a great deal of stress."

After you finish your summation, assume that the owners are sold on you, your firm, and having you represent them. It is time to complete the final preparations for the closing.

The Trial Closing. A trial closing on a listing consists simply of asking a question or giving the owners a choice which presumes a closing. Their answer really is an agreement to list their property with you:

"Would you be able to give the buyers possession within 30 days?"

"How long would you need to give the buyers possession? Thirty days is the usual time. Would this be convenient for you?"

"Would you want my firm to represent you for 90 days or a 120-day period?"

The last question gives the owner one of two choices. The owners will most likely say 90 days. Whenever you give choices, you should have an idea as to what choice the owners are likely to make. You wanted a 90-day listing so your choice was 90 days or 120 days. If you had said 60 or 90 days, the owner would want 60 days.

If you gave an undirected question such as, "How long do you want to give our firm to sell your home?" you are asking for trouble. First of all you are asking the owner to "give you" something. Never ask the owner to give; that is not a benefit. You are the one giving by representing the owner; that is a benefit. An owner asked a question phrased this way is likely to resist a listing, or to give you 10 or 20 days. This puts you in the position of having to convince the owners that you need more time. Providing a properly directed choice will avoid such problems.

The Pre-prepared Agreement. One way to upset owners is to open a briefcase and take out a listing form before the owners are ready for it. I don't like briefcases. Filling in information on a form on a clipboard seems natural and far less threatening than opening a briefcase and taking out a listing contract. If you wish to carry a briefcase for your presentation material, consider carrying a clipboard in it to remove early in the presentation.

Your trial closing questions will complete the information you need for the listing form, which has already been filled in with the data you used in your competitive market analysis. Never delay a listing because you lack information. If you don't have lien balances, for example, you can indicate that they will be supplied.

A Last Little Push. When your listing form is complete, you are ready for the actual closing, which is really very simple. All you have to do is hand the owners the listing and pen and say,

"Please approve our agreement where I have indicated."

Let the owners take their time with the pen in their hand. Because people are accustomed to signing things, signing is almost a reflex with many people. I have had owners who told me just before I gave them the listing that "We definitely are not going to list today." Then they took the pen I handed them and signed the agreement.

Some owners will hesitate, but don't mistake reading for hesitation. Don't interrupt if they are reading over the agreement, but if they tighten their grip on the pen instead of signing, or look away from the agreement, a little push is in order.

You might use a newspaper advertising deadline as a push:

> "The deadline for weekend ads is tomorrow morning. I have prepared some ads on your home. [Hand them to the owners]. I will have them at the newspaper tomorrow morning and we can have an Open House this Sunday."

Another final push is to hand the owners a model of the multiple listing form you have prepared, including a Polaroid photo of the house:

> "Tomorrow this information will be on the way to 800 real estate salespeople in 53 offices."

If an owner is planning a move to Florida, you can inspire action with this:

> "Let's try to have you in Florida by Christmas."

A salesperson with a strong outgoing personality might get results this way:

> "Some owners feel I come on too strong. Actually I am quite subdued now compared to how I am with buyers. An owner in Sunnyside Estates told me that he chose me to represent him because he would rather have me working on buyers *for* him than working *on* him. Incidentally, I was successful in selling his home. By approving this agreement, you will have me working on your team."

A friend of mine uses the following clincher:

"Right now you are worried about selling your home; that's understandable. Now, you could hire someone to worry for you but that won't sell your house. You must hire someone who not only can but *will* sell your house. And you're doing that right now."

Some people don't like to be that positive, but I feel strongly that if you don't fully believe you will sell the property, you should not be taking the listing as written.

A Power clincher I like for tough owners who have a sense of humor is:

"Mr. Jones, you are one of the strongest owners I have ever encountered. By strong I mean that I don't think anyone has ever been able to get you to do anything you weren't sure was in your best interests. After working with you, the hardest part is over. I look forward to selling your home because, by comparison, convincing a buyer to buy will be easy."

Most owners will like this image you have given them. This compliment has resulted in many owners laughing as they sign the agreement.

Never threaten owners. Warning them that you will take a prospective buyer elsewhere unless they sign will only anger them. No one likes a threat, even an implied one, whether it be physical or financial. A threat can turn a likely listing situation into an owners' decision to have nothing to do with your firm.

Last-Minute Objections. If an owner puts down the pen, there is an objection. Unfortunately, some objections are not raised until the very last minute. Before you get the listing signed, you must identify the objection and overcome it.

To determine the problem, you can simply ask:

"Do you have any questions about our agreement?"

If the owners indicate there are none, state:

"You seem to be hesitant. If something is bothering you, I would very much like to know."

Don't use the term *problem* or *objection,* as these are negative words.

When you discover the owners' objection, try to establish that this is the source of the hesitation:

> "Let me rephrase what you have said. If it were not for_____
> and _____you would want me to represent you in the sale
> of your home. Is that correct?"

The response will be positive to this type of question. "You
would want me to represent you," is a very positive statement.

You now must overcome the objections presented
(Chapter 6).

When you feel you have overcome the objections, go
back to your closing statements:

> "I believe that I have answered your questions; now let's get
> your house sold."

Pick up the pen and listing and hand them once again to
the owners.

As long as you have an owner listening to you, keep
going after the listing. You cannot try for a closing too many
times. It may take handing the listing and pen to the owner
six or eight times before you finally get a signature. If the
owner still has the listing but has put down the pen, give him
or her another one with each closing attempt.

Overcoming Delaying Tactics. Many people are procrastinators.
They want to postpone making a commitment with the
excuse, "I would like to think it over." In dealing with
owners who want to delay a listing decision, you need a
way to lead them back to an agreement:

> "What is there that bothers you?"

> "Do you want to sell your home?"

> "Do you want as quick a sale as possible?"

> "Do you want to receive fair value for your home?"

"Do you agree that the competitive market analysis I have prepared is realistic?"

"Have I convinced you that my firm is competent to handle the sale of your home?"

"If this is the case, let's get your house sold."

This sequence of questions calling for *yes* answers leads right to a closing. Hand the owner the listing and a pen.

This approach makes a strong point of the relief the owners will feel once they've made their decision:

"What can I tell you? If there are any questions you may have, I would like to know. Only by complete honesty can we work together. There is nothing you will know tomorrow that you don't know now. The fact that you want to sell now is the best reason for letting me represent you, starting now. I can't start working for you until you let me.

Instead of worrying about what you should do to sell your home, wouldn't it be better to go to bed tonight knowing I'm the one who will be doing your worrying for you? Actually, I will be doing a lot more than worrying. I will be starting a campaign that is going to result in the sale of your property. By giving me the go-ahead, you can get a good night's sleep.

This presentation also ends with your handing the owners a listing and pen.

WHEN THE LISTING IS SIGNED

Once the listing has been signed, thank the owners and leave their home, making sure you have left a copy of the listing. I recommend you fold the listing and put it in an envelope for the owners.

If you consider the listing price a little high, but you agree to test the market, you want the owners to fully understand that a price adjustment might become necessary:

"You, not I, set the price. After all, you are the owners and my job is to represent you. I feel the price is a little high; however,

I will do my best to find a buyer at your price. If we are not successful, we can evaluate the price later based upon the comments of prospective buyers."

A successful listing starts the chain of events leading to a sale. It has often been said, "A property well listed is half sold." If this statement is not entirely true, it is because well-listed property probably goes more than halfway to the final sale.

SERVICING THE LISTING

Many real estate salespeople interpret "servicing the listing" to mean convincing owners to reduce the price. Some seminars even cover techniques for "working the owners down" after they have entered into the listing. It takes a lot of chutzpah to call this servicing the listing. Is this doing a service to the owners? It is not necessarily in the owners' best interests to reduce the price. This is especially true for properties having limited appeal, where finding a qualified buyer with specific needs is more important than a simple price reduction.

Servicing the listing really means working and communicating with the owners for the owners' best interests. Selling takes a team approach, and the owners must realize that they are an important part of the team. Their actions can help effectuate a successful sale.

Following are steps that will keep the owners' good will and help them to do their part in setting up a successful sale.

Signs. Usually the first act in servicing the listing is putting up the For Sale sign. Owners expect a sign, and signs actually are the most cost-effective advertising a broker can get. The ratio of inquiries per dollar invested in signs far exceeds other forms of advertising. Salespeople usually carry signs in their cars and put one up immediately upon taking the listing.

Some offices have large impressive signs which take several people to erect. If your office does this, put up a small sign for temporary use. The owner should be told when and where the large sign will be in place. When you feature a property on your office billboard, call the owners and let them know what you are doing for them.

Keeping Owners Informed. Many brokers have "thank you" cards with their firm name and logo printed on them. Brokers often use these cards to send a short handwritten note to the owners thanking them for employing the broker as agent for the sale of their property, as well as promising to use one's best efforts in the owner's behalf.

The First Meeting. I recommend you meet with your owners one or two days after the listing is taken. Inform them about what your office has done and will be doing, and what is expected of them. After this first post-listing meeting, you should plan on contacting your owners at least once a week to keep them fully informed about your activities, interest in their property, and any changes in market conditions.

Market Opinion. If there is a lock box on occupied property, check with your owners periodically for cards left by other salespeople. Contact these salespeople for their prospects' comments and interests. This information should then be supplied to the owner. For vacant property, a sign-in sheet will record the names and offices of other agents, and the date of showing.

Notice of Showings. The owners should be notified prior to showings. Try to give them at least an hour's notice. If for some reason a showing is cancelled, call the owners and explain. After showings, let the owners know the reactions of the prospective buyers. Comments often reveal the need to fix some fault or adjust the price.

What the Owners Get. At the time you took the listing you probably gave the owners a verbal estimate of their net sale proceeds. As soon as possible after taking the listing, prepare a detailed written worksheet showing what they can expect to realize from a sale at the list price. Consider impound account balances, insurance, and all costs. Try to be accurate. Brokers who give overly optimistic figures create animosity when they are proven wrong.

If the price is later adjusted, you'll have to figure a new estimate. Many firms and organizations have their own forms for this purpose. The "Estimated Seller's Proceeds" form on the next page is the standard form of the California Association of Realtors ® . The same form can be completed and presented with an offer to show the implications of an offered price.

Selected Buyers vs. the Crowd. You should explain to the owners that you will be qualifying all prospective buyers, so there will be no crowds of prospects looking at the house. You are not interested in numbers, but in the one prospect who will be the next owner of the property. Explain that the number of people who view the property may be smaller than the number that the owners' signs and advertisements attracted.

Explain Your Ads. You can expect your owners to closely monitor your ads. They expect to see their property constantly displayed in a prominent fashion. When it isn't they'll be disappointed. Explain that it is not necessary to advertise a property every day. Similar property being advertised will produce prospects for their property, just as ads on their property will attract prospective buyers for other properties. Put a copy of every ad on the property in its listing file, and send copies of all ads to the owners.

Instructions to Owners. Some offices have prepared owner instruction books such as *Working Together to Sell Your Home.* Should you use a booklet, an owner check sheet, or simply handle it verbally, owner instructions can make or break a sale. The owners must realize that their property is in direct competition with many others. They must help you to create a competitive advantage for their home.

Let the owners know what to do if a prospect comes to the door. Even with your sign out front, buyers will do this. Tell the owners to get the name and phone number of the prospects and call you right away. Have them ask the prospects to wait until you arrive.

Out of Sight . . . . I feel that the most important instruction to the owner is to be as unobtrusive as possible.

ESTIMATED SELLER'S PROCEEDS
California Association of Realtors® Standard Form

SELLER _____

PROPERTY ADDRESS _____

BROKER _____

This estimate is based on costs associated with _____ financing.   ESTIMATED CLOSING DATE _____

PROJECTED SELLING PRICE $ _____

ENCUMBRANCES

First Trust Deed	$ _____
Second Trust Deed	_____
Other Encumbrances	_____
TOTAL	$ _____

PROJECTED GROSS EQUITY $ _____

ESTIMATED COSTS

		ESTIMATED CREDITS	
Escrow	$ _____	Prorated Taxes	$ _____
Sub Escrow	_____	Prorated Insurance	_____
Recording	_____	Prorated Rents	_____
Drawing Deed	_____	Impound Accounts	_____
Title Insurance	_____	Other	_____
Transfer Tax	_____	Other	_____
Notary	_____		
Pre-Payment Penalty	_____		
Forwarding or Transfer	_____		
Reconveyance	_____		
Interest	_____		
Discount @ %	_____	TOTAL ESTIMATED COSTS $ _____	
Preparation of Documents	_____	LESS ESTIMATED CREDITS $ _____	
Taxes	_____		
Appraisal	_____	NET SELLER'S COSTS $ _____	
Structural Pest Control Inspection	_____	PURCHASE MONEY NOTE	
Structural Pest Control Repairs	_____	(if any) _____	
FHA-VA or Lender	_____	ESTIMATED SELLER'S	
Home Warrantee	_____	CASH PROCEEDS $ _____	
Brokerage	_____		
Buyer's Fees	_____		
Miscellaneous Fees	_____		
TOTAL	$ _____		

This estimate based upon the above projected selling price, type of financing, and estimated closing dates, has been prepared to assist the seller in computing his costs. Lenders and escrow companies will vary in their charges; therefore, these figures cannot be guaranteed by the broker or his representatives.

I have read the above figures and acknowledge receipt of a copy of this form.

Presented by: _____

Seller _____ Date _____   Address: _____

_____ Date _____   Phone No.: _____

The estimated seller's proceeds calculated above will vary according to any difference in unpaid loan balances, bonds assessments, other liens, impound account, if any, and any expenses for required repairs. All estimates and information are from sources believed reliable but not guaranteed.

For these forms address — California Association of Realtors®
505 Shatto Place, Los Angeles, California 90020
Copyright © 1978, California Association of Realtors®   **FORM ESP-II**

If they must be present at the time of a showing, they should fade into the background after being introduced to the prospective buyers. I strongly recommend *telling* the owners to leave the house when they are notified it is to be shown.

Explain that prospective buyers will seldom communicate their objections if an owner is present, and unspoken objections cannot be overcome. Also, prospects feel uncomfortable poking into closets and other areas if the owners are present. If you are to turn the prospects into buyers, it is essential that they be able to picture the property as belonging to them. That is unlikely when the owners are present.

It's their home, so owners often resist being told to leave, even with the explanations given. If an owner insists on remaining, consider the following Power approach:

> "By being present in the house, a prospective buyer will feel your anxiety to sell, which is natural. If a buyer feels owners are anxious to sell, the buyer is likely to reduce any offer he or she might otherwise have made, as well as take a very hard position in subsequent bargaining."

If the owners are unable to leave, they must understand that they are not to volunteer any information. Otherwise they will interrupt a well-planned sales approach. They might also give information that turns off the buyer. When the elderly owner tells prospective buyers that there are no children in the area, he or she may feel an important plus has been added. The young couple planning on starting a family will not see it that way.

Children. Suggest to the owner that children be sent out to play or to a friend's house when the home is to be shown. Children, though they may be well-behaved, can distract prospective purchasers.

Pets. Pets should be outside during a showing. They may be cute and well-behaved, but they, too, will distract a prospective buyer. It is the house, not the pet, you want to sell. Pet odors should be camouflaged with spray if necessary. The yard should be clean of animal dirt. Stepping in the wrong place could kill a sale very quickly.

Preparing the Property. Another important job for the owners
is getting the property ready to look its best. Though they
may normally be excellent housekeepers, owners who have
been in a house for a long time tend to overlook things
they've learned to live with. It is up to you to point out
what needs changing, and to bring up these delicate matters
without offending your clients.

Housekeeping. Rather than tell owners they are terrible
housekeepers, explain that this is a special case:

> "We are competing against brand-new units that have never
> been lived in. Buyers today are accustomed to seeing model
> units. Your home should look as if people didn't live here. The
> lived-in look is out. Used car dealers "detail" their cars. What
> this means is they try to make them look as much like new as
> possible. It works; it sells cars. The same holds true for homes.
> The more they look as if they were never lived in, the easier
> they sell."

Beds must be made up and closets spruced up. Most
closets are overloaded. Suggest that the owners put some
of their things in boxes and store them in the basement or
garage. An overstuffed closet will make the storage space
seem inadequate.

Basements and garages should be clean and cleared. All
that good stuff the owners are saving should be put away in
boxes. Tools should be in neat array. A neat basement or
garage looks larger than a cluttered one.

Many houses have far too much furniture, which makes
a room look small and unappealing. Suggest moving out
some pieces and storing them at a mini-warehouse. Carpets
should be professionally shampooed, and worn furniture
given throws or slipcovers.

Urge that floors be stripped and waxed, and appliances
shined with car wax. Torn shades should be replaced. If new
draperies are needed, I recommend light-colored, inexpensive,
foam-lined drapes. They appear far more expensive than
they really are.

Odors can have powerful effects on sale efforts. Recommend that the owners avoid heavy frying and strong-smelling food like garlic, cabbage, and pickling with vinegar. The smell of fresh bread, cookies or cinnamon, on the other hand, conjures up real or imagined memories of happy childhoods. One broker advises owners to buy refrigerated packages of chocolate chip cookie dough and to start baking whenever they are notified their home is to be shown.

In winter have your owners start a fire in the fireplace before a showing. This will convey a warm atmosphere which is very conducive to a sale. In summer the air conditioning should be set a little cooler than normal before a showing. Coming from the heat into a cool home will leave a very favorable impression on the prospective buyers.

An FM station turned down low can be beneficial, but keep television sets off. You don't want your buyers watching a soap opera or a ball game; you want them interested in the house.

Draperies should be pulled open for maximum light and lights should be on. Dark rooms are depressing, and you don't want a depressed prospect.

Improvements and Repairs. Go through the house with the owners and make suggestions. Often every $50 in maintenance can mean $100 or more in the sales price.

• If walls need repainting or repairs, say so. Recommend light colors to make rooms appear larger.

• If the exterior needs repainting, it might only be the trim. The south and west sides of a building show the worst weathering. If the paint can be properly matched, just the one or two worst sides can be painted.

• The bath and kitchen must sparkle. Often an inexpensive new lighting fixture can change the appearance of a room. If a bath has a tiny old-fashioned medicine cabinet, suggest a large new mirrored cabinet with fluorescent lights.

• A stained or broken toilet seat should be replaced. Any loose tile should be repaired. The bath area might require new grouting around the tub. Perhaps a new colorful shower curtain will help.

• The owner might have grown used to a gurgling toilet or a dripping faucet; these should be fixed now.

• In these days of energy conservation, many people have gone to lower-wattage bulbs in lamps and light fixtures. I suggest the wattage be increased where necessary to make the rooms as bright as possible. Light fixtures should be cleaned.

• Front doors often need refinishing or repainting. They are the first thing a prospective buyer sees, so see that they give a good first impression.

• Doors and cabinets that stick or don't close right should be adjusted.

• Flowers in bloom have presold many buyers before they entered the house. The lawn should also be neat and trim.

• Most people dream about growing things but never do. A small vegetable garden can be the answer to a buyer's dream.

• Several small fruit trees are also a plus. Many supermarkets sell bare root fruit trees for about $10 each.

• If an owner does not intend to leave an item which would normally remain, such as a light fixture, have it removed and replaced right away. Otherwise you could have trouble when a new owner notices the fixture missing.

Once I went to extend a listing on a house where I had made numerous suggestions for improvements and repairs both inside and outside. My owners had been very cooperative—they had created a remarkable change. I received two offers that failed because of financing problems, but was certain I would have it sold shortly.

My owners, to my astonishment, refused the extension. They no longer wanted to sell. After fixing the place up, they realized what a nice home they had after all and how well it really suited their needs. I consider this a success story even without a sale. I did meet the needs of the owners.

Electricity. Owners will want to disconnect the electricity when they vacate a home. They should understand that initial showings are often after working hours, which can mean after dark. Not being able to show the property then could mean the loss of a sale opportunity. Keep the electricity on.

Controlling Access. To show property, you need the keys. Don't accept "I'm always home," or "The neighbor has it." Murphy's law says, "Whatever can go wrong will go wrong," and O'Brien's law says, "Murphy was an optimist." As soon as you find the ideal buyers, expect the owners and the neighbors to pull a disappearing act.

The Lock Box. A lock box is simply a locked container holding a key. It is usually locked to the front door handle. The lock box can be opened with a combination or a special key which the members of your listing service have.

Always get the owner to agree to a lock box on vacant property. Lock boxes mean more showings. Often prospects' reactions to other property indicate that they might be interested in this one. A lock box allows you to show it without a special trip for the keys that might cool prospect interest. A lock box also makes entry possible when offices are closed, such as evenings and Sunday afternoons.

Security. While I recommend lock boxes on occupied units, I also recommend that owners not leave cash or other small valuables around. The owners should be informed of both the dangers and advantages of lock boxes. Have the owners agree in writing to the installation of the lock box, explaining that you or another agent will call prior to showing the home, but would like to show the property when the owners are not available. Tell them that the agent will ring the doorbell prior to entry and will leave his or her card before leaving. In homes having very valuable furnishings or art objects, a lock box may not be wise. Items have disappeared in homes with these devices.

You are liable for negligence. Don't give a key or combination to any unauthorized person. Protect keys and combinations. Because of possible lock box liability, you need adequate insurance. Normal errors and omissions policies are not adequate, as they do not cover property in the care or control of the broker. A broad-form property endorsement can be added to protect the broker.

Being Ready With Facts. Once you have the listing, you need information from various sources in order to be able to advise owners as well as prospects about the best options and procedures available to them. Here are the major areas to keep track of.

Financing. If secondary financing might be required, contact a mortgage broker to determine the amount and terms that are possible. This information, along with a lender appraisal, puts you in a strong position to influence a prospective buyer, compared with an agent who is only guessing.

You might want to advise an owner to obtain information on refinancing an existing loan to reduce equity. Check the balances and assumability of all existing loans, as owners are often confused. Ask for the lender's statement the owners received at the end of the year. It is likely to be with their income tax material.

If a loan is not assumable, see whether there are any prepayment penalties. Even if there are, a lender sometimes waives it when the existing loan is at a below-market interest rate. Usually this is done only if the lender is asked in advance.

Appraisals. If an FHA or VA appraisal is to be obtained, collect the appraisal fee from the owners in advance. You should alert the owners that often these appraisals seem a little high at the low end of the spectrum, but may undervalue very expensive property.

You may encounter an FHA appraisal that requires what you consider a ridiculous corrective action. I have been amazed at the conditions attached by some appraisers. If you have been having problems with FHA appraisals in your area, you should alert the owner about what to expect.

Appraisals could indicate that the price needs adjustment. If you expect a home to sell at $32,000 with FHA financing and the FHA appraises it at $31,200, you should suggest to the owners that the price be adjusted to the appraisal.

Insurance. You need to know about insurance coverage, cost, and expiration date, as well as the agent's name. It is in the owners' best interests that buyers assume the insurance rather than cancel it and take out their own policy. With assumption of the policy, your owners get a prorated settlement and thus full credit for prepaid but unused coverage. If the policy is cancelled, your owners get a short-rate refund which is considerably less than a prorated amount.

Zoning. For other than single-family homes, check the zoning to make sure it is as stated. Checking the zoning map might reveal possible changes which could increase buyer interest.

Restrictions. Copies of subdivision or condominium restrictions should be obtained so they can be available to prospective buyers.

Termite Inspection. If you anticipate that a structural and pest control certificiate will be required, arrange for the inspection with owners' concurrence. This might reveal problems that have to be cured.

Bonds. If there are unpaid improvement bonds against the property, the balances should be ascertained.

Market Update. You might want to perform another competitive market analysis based upon the latest sales. Your listing might be based on yesterday's market. In a rising market it could be in the owner's best interest to increase the list price, but in a falling market a downward adjustment might be necessary.

Again, never use the term *price reduction*, since you are not reducing anything. Reducing indicates you are taking something away. In a price adjustment you are not taking anything away from the buyers that they had before. You are simply setting a more realistic price based upon a reevaluation of the property and market conditions.

GETTING THE INFORMATION OUT

As soon as you put up your sign, you can expect phone calls from prospective buyers as well as other agents. You must make certain the listing information is immediately available to all salespeople in your office.

As soon as you have prepared the MLS listing, send a copy to the owners. Often it can take one to two weeks from the time a listing is taken until it is received from the MLS service by the other members of the service. One way to arouse special interest is to personally drop off copies of the listing information at a few offices that specialize in that area, type of property, and/or price range, and to inform a few particularly successful agents. Brokers and salespeople tend to give special attention to these advance listings, since they are getting a few days' jump on their competition. If you give a listing this special treatment, make certain the owners know what you are doing for them.

Some agents take their time in distributing what they consider good listings. They don't submit the data to their multiple listing service until they have to, hoping to sell these listings themselves without a commission split. Such a practice is, of course, unethical since it is not working in the best interests of the owners to effect a quick sale. Failure to distribute listings promptly is also poor business practice because other brokers will quickly realize how you do business. If you later push a particular listing, other agents will know you are doing so because you consider the listing a "dog."

Agent Open House. If you have a listing for an unusual property or a number of properties, such as a group of homes or condominium units from a builder, you might consider an open house just for real estate professionals. A champagne party with formal invitations to other brokers and salespeople is an inexpensive way to publicize a property and to get others interested in selling. Invite the real estate editors of local papers as well as your owners. Have handout material ready of a size that fits the local listing books.

You will be amazed at how many salespeople show up for a few free glasses of champagne and a few hors d'oeuvres. Some agent open houses offer door prizes as an added inducement. Owners greatly appreciate this type of special promotion.

 **FOR BROKERS & AGENTS**
1827 BOLTON STREET
APRIL 20th 1-4 P.M.

❦ **REFRESHMENTS SERVED** ❦

IN HISTORIC BOLTON HILL. THIS HOUSE HAS NUMEROUS SURPRISES!
COME SEE AND YOU WILL BE SOLD!   MLS 47653-4

WIN A FREE WEEK-END FOR TWO
at the
SHERATON HILTON, WASHINGTON, D.C.

CLYDE REALTY

Property Brief. Besides preparing the information about a property for a multiple listing service, consider preparing a property brief like the one on the next page. A brief is used for
mailings to prospective buyers and other brokers, and as an
enclosure when answering inquiries. It can be given to
prospective buyers after a showing and to other salespeople
after a caravan. The brief is full of adjectives describing the
property and should include a photograph, or even better,
a drawing. A map or directions to the property might also
be included in the brief.

Open House. Should you have an open house, invite the neighbors, call other prospects, invite other brokers. Owners like
open houses because they can see that their house is receiving
special treatment. After any open house, discuss the results
with the owners.

Neighbors. If you send letters out to neighbors inviting them to
help choose their new neighbors, send a copy to the owners.
Consider personally canvassing the area of the listing and
making sure the owners know of your efforts.

EXTENDING THE LISTING

Several weeks before the listing is to expire, you should make
an appointment with the owners to review their property and
what you have done. Cover in detail what you have done
since the property was listed, including financing arrangements, multiple listings distribution, advertising, showings,
etc. Suggest any further changes in price, terms, or condition of property.

With that settled, bring up the question of the listing
time:

"Our agency agreement expires on _____. Don't you
think I deserve an extended opportunity to help you?"

You are more likely to get a positive response with " . . .
deserve an extended opportunity to help you," than with
"Will you give me an extension?" If the owners feel you

ROLAND PARK
"Restored to Original Elegance"

MLS#
68190-1

5500 Lombardy Place • Baltimore, Maryland 21210

5 bedroom, 3½ bath stone English Country Manor residence situated on a private court location. Home features a sunken living room (23.3' x 16.6') with massive stone fireplace and built-in cabinets, large formal dining room (28.3' x 12.6') with built-in china cabinets, crystal chandelier and custom mouldings, sunken den (15.6' x 10.6') with french doors leading to screened enclosed porch (17.6' x 11.6'), modernized kitchen with breakfast room and powder room. Master bedroom suite with dressing room and full bath and 4 additional bedrooms, family bath and sun deck on second floor. Many unique features such as brass hardware, rebuilt and insulated windows, re-plastered and repainted walls throughout, all stone sandblasted, repointed and siliconed, new back porch, hardwood floors refinished, a 2 zoned alarm system and abundance of insulation. A RARE OFFERING.

Offered at $179,000   *SPECIAL FINANCING*

DIRECTIONS: Roland Ave. to west on Northern Parkway to north on Lombardy Place.

Sales By: **CLYDE REALTY**   **476-8200**

EQUAL HOUSING
OPPORTUNITY

Adapted with permission, Central Maryland Multiple Listing Service, Inc.

have been fair with them, have communicated with them, and have really been trying, then you can expect an extension.

You should have the completed extension agreement ready to hand to the owners with a pen for their "approval." If the owners want to know why you have come several weeks prior to expiration, you can explain that a listing extension takes time to process through your multiple listing service. You want to make sure that the extension is distributed before the property is taken off the market as an expired listing.

The most common reason owners do not extend listings is lack of communication. The owners often feel forgotten after a listing has been taken. If you have followed the suggestions in this chapter, lack of communication should not be your problem. Should the owners have to call you to find out what's happening, you are not doing your job.

THE SALE

A detailed summary of the selling process, including presenting offers for acceptance, is the subject of my companion volume, *Power Real Estate Selling.*

Sold! When an offer is accepted, put up a Sold sign and ask the owners to please leave it up until the new owners move in. This evidence of success will make it much easier to obtain other listings in the area, and add credibility to your assertion that you excell at selling property.

If there is a problem after an offer has been accepted, keep the owners informed. Some real estate salespeople don't want to be the bearers of bad news, so they delay telling the owners, hoping the problem will be solved. In the meantime, the owners could be obligating themselves based upon what they believe is a definite sale.

Some offices have checklists for their agents of things to be done prior to settlement. Checklists are far better than just memory.

Ask the owners to:

• leave all keys, including any spares;

• label and leave any matching paint they have, as it will be of no value to them elsewhere;

• leave service manuals and warranties as applicable;

• make certain they have notified all utilities to be cancelled or transferred.

If additional cash will be required for closing, check with the attorney or escrow and inform the buyer of the exact requirements.

Help the Buyer. Ask the neighbors to welcome the new buyer to the area. Provide a map as well as phone and utility service numbers. Your new buyers can become leads for future business and will eventually be sellers. If you help them settle into their new location, they will be your sellers.

Just the Beginning

Each sale should be viewed not as an end but rather as another new beginning. Real estate sales are not isolated transactions that stand alone. Each is part of a chain of related listings and sales, and you are a vital link. Sellers will become buyers in the future and then sellers again. Your circle of success goes far beyond those individuals, however. Your success can extend to a wide association of their friends and acquaintances. Successfully meeting the needs of individuals will open the doors of many homes.

If you are relatively new to real estate sales, this book, along with its companion, *Power Real Estate Selling*, will provide you with a complete course in real estate listings and sales. If you are an experienced salesperson, it is hoped that these books have stimulated you by providing a multitude of successful traditional and non traditional ideas.

As you study and apply the ideas presented here, remember that there is no one true path to success in real estate. There are as many approaches as there are unique personalities, so find the ideas and methods that you feel comfortable and effective using, and concentrate on applying them to the best of your ability. Once you've found the approach that is right for you, your new confidence will enable you to do your best for your clients, and will inspire positive attitudes in the people around you. But the right route cannot do the job by itself. To travel it successfully will require your full attention, work, and dedication. *Bon Voyage.*